BEAUTY BY DESIGN

For Linda —

With our thanks for sharing your wonderful garden, your ideas and your stories —.

Brian Leny. & Rosemary Bates.

AUGUST 2013

BEAUTY *by* DESIGN

INSPIRED GARDENING IN THE PACIFIC NORTHWEST

BILL TERRY & ROSEMARY BATES

TouchWood Editions
touchwoodeditions.com

LIBRARY AND ARCHIVES CANADA CATALOGUING IN PUBLICATION
Terry, Bill, 1935–
Beauty by design : inspired gardening in the Pacific Northwest / Bill Terry, Rosemary Bates.

Issued in print and electronic formats.
ISBN 978-1-77151-012-7

1. Gardens—Northwest, Pacific—Design. I. Bates, Rosemary, 1947–

SB473.T47 2013 712'.6 C2013-902046-2

Editor: Marlyn Horsdal
Proofreader: Vivian Sinclair
Design: Pete Kohut
Cover images by Bill Terry except tall foxtail lilies (front cover) by Linda Cochran and autumn colour (back cover) by Judi Dyelle.
Interior images by Bill Terry unless annotated.
Poems on pages 125–126 and 131–132 excerpted from *The Blue Hour of the Day: Selected Poems* by Lorna Crozier. Copyright © 2007 Lorna Crozier. Reprinted by permission of McClelland & Stewart.

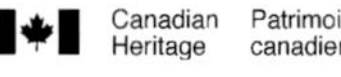

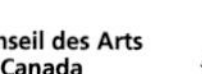

We gratefully acknowledge the financial support for our publishing activities from the Government of Canada through the Canada Book Fund, Canada Council for the Arts, and the province of British Columbia through the British Columbia Arts Council and the Book Publishing Tax Credit.

This book was produced using FSC®-certified, acid-free paper, processed chlorine free and printed with soya-based inks.

1 2 3 4 5 17 16 15 14 13

PRINTED IN CHINA

For our children:
John, Daniel, Christina, Sarah, Hilary

The rough textures of fir bark and a concrete mask are softly entwined with ivy in Robin Hopper's garden.

Contents

Saturated blue: *Meconopsis* 'Lingholm' in Linda Cochran's garden.

Consult the genius of the place in all;
That tells the waters or to rise, or fall;
Or helps th' ambitious hill the heav'ns to scale,
Or scoops in circling theatres the vale;
Calls in the country, catches opening glades,
Joins willing woods, and varies shades from shades,
Now breaks, or now directs, th' intending lines;
Paints as you plant, and, as you work, designs.

—Alexander Pope[1]

Niellia thibetica in Eva Diener's garden.

Introduction

"CONSULT THE *GENIUS* OF THE place in all," advised Alexander Pope, the eighteenth-century English poet and designer of gardens. He was using "genius" in a sense that would have been understood in those days to mean the natural spirit of the setting, its essential character. Consider, he urged, "in all," the rise and fall of the terrain, the views beyond, the watery reflections in stream or pond, the rock, the trees, the transit of the sun across the sky.

Today, far less eloquently, we might be advised to "scope out the lay of the land" before laying a hand on axe or shovel.

From the many outstanding private gardens in the Pacific Northwest, we have chosen eleven. We have chosen them for their standing as (yes) works of art and also, in many cases, for their interplay with other arts—painting, pottery, photography, poetry, sculpture, even theatre. The gardens express different styles and different tastes but, in common, all have been created by gardeners who have consulted "the genius of the place in all," who are therefore very much aware of the landscape within which they work, and who usually seek a unifying theme.

For these people, gardening is much, much more than a hobby. It's a passionate pursuit of perfection. They also acknowledge that that perfection is, like the end of the rainbow, forever just beyond reach, and that a garden is, and always will be, a *work in progress*.

Their tastes and choices have been shaped and focussed by experience and observation. None would refer to the garden as a "yard"—believing, as we do, that a yard is a place for chickens to run about in, or maybe for hanging out the laundry. There are farmyards, graveyards, schoolyards, churchyards, brickyards, scrapyards, shipyards, and prison yards. Usually, none of these is a garden. *Courtyards*, however, as we discovered, may be gardens of enchantment.

These gardeners, indeed *all* gardeners, are alchemists of nature, art, and artifice. As Des Kennedy said to us, "I think gardeners are a whole subset of the human race. They are primarily engaged in the creation of beauty, with a delighted sense of what's important in life. Beauty is important and growth is important and creativity is important. Gardeners are like an artistic community and, by and large, a generous and unpretentious one as well, ever ready to say, 'My garden isn't what I'd like it to be right now, but your garden is wonderful.'"

During the two and a half years of bringing this book from proposal to print, we have found that the passion of these gardeners has rubbed off; our insights have been honed, our senses better tuned. We have sharpened our appreciation of shades of green: foliage in its variation of form, size, and colour in all seasons. We are more inclined to look beyond the flowers to include in our view the texture of bark, the curve of a bough, the wonder of a seed pod, the overall *balance*. We see, where we might not have seen before, the etched patterns of moss and lichen on granite. From the gardens we have had the privilege of visiting, and our immersion in the ideas of those who paint as they plant, we have also observed the value of letting nature take its course—within limits—and the resulting delight of welcoming serendipity, the happy accident, as a partner in the garden.

We hope that readers will share our delight in visiting these gardens and meeting the people who create beauty by design.

The metallic sheen of a clay pot gleams through rattling seed heads in Kathy Leishman's garden.

Southwest, across the Salish Sea.

ONE

A Garden for All Seasons

"GARDENING IS AN ART. YES. It *is* an art, but it can be learned. We can't all be opera singers because it's not there. It's a stretch for me to sing Christmas carols without making everyone cringe. But I feel that anyone who wants to garden and is determined to do it well can do the research, can learn the necessary science about soil conditions and so on, can explore and define how they want their garden to be—and then make it happen. I think it's one of the most freeing of artistic expressions. I think it should be fun too."

So says Kathy Leishman, an outstanding, creative gardener, respected throughout the Pacific Northwest for her knowledge of plants and her skill and innovation in choosing just the right bedmates for them. The art, she insists, is not innate but *learned*: learned from careful observation of other gardens, from paying close attention to the experience of expert plant people, and from books.

She refers to a typical *eureka!* moment: "A turning point for me as a gardener was when my mother and I went on one of David Tarrant's trips to southern England and we went to Sissinghurst, the garden of Vita Sackville-West. Well, I can tell you right now, it was like having a whole garden education in one day. I was so blown away I could hardly stand it. I took tons of pictures and that's when I said to myself, 'Oh, I could have a yellow border, I could have a white garden.' It was at the end of May and Sissinghurst opened my eyes to how to use perennials in an overall design, for repetition, for contrast, such as a delphinium with a peony, the spike and the round shape."

Fish out of water.

We first saw Kathy's waterfront garden on Bowen Island in mid-January.

In front of the house, the sea reflected steel-grey clouds and a watery sun. In the foreground, rusty iron fish appeared to float lazily through the reeds. Beyond, tall plumes of grass waved at occasional passing tugs hauling barge-loads of sawdust. Relics that others might have consigned to the compost pile with the fall cleanup, such as the dried seed heads of sea holly (*Eryngium planum*) and Jerusalem sage (*Phlomis fruticosa*), were left to rattle in the wind, bearing witness to the idea that, in winter, there is still life and colour in these dead forms.

"In fall," notes Kathy, "I skip the cleanup and leave the dead stems if the structures look good, like the dried sedum or the oregano. They're part of the *volume*. It makes it all fit together. Besides, in the front, there's often little birds scurrying about, and they love the seeds."

The garden in winter.

There was movement too, especially in the soft shivering of the willowy grasses. Dead strands of oregano muted the hard edges of a gorgeous, blue-green stoneware pot. And to top it off, in contrast to all this subtlety, a majestic old-growth Douglas fir stands guard near the water's edge—a favourite lookout for bald eagles. Like everything in the garden, it looked perfectly natural. In fact, this stately tree had been spirally pruned in order to maintain the essence of its architecture—straight trunk and heavy boughs—while letting in light and opening the view southwest across the Salish Sea to distant Vancouver Island.

Behind the house, it was quieter. The first snowdrop was in bloom. A trace of snow had fallen overnight. Most of it had melted away, leaving soft, white brush strokes on the variegated leaves of a New Zealand pittosporum and the flower buds of *Skimmia japonica*. A whiff of witch hazel (*Hamamelis mollis*) was in the air. The royal grevillea (*Grevillea victoriae*) was hanging out its orange-red tresses. It is the only species of this evergreen Australian native that is reliably hardy in the Pacific Northwest.

Seldom is so much attention given to the appearance of a garden in winter.

Looking out the window in midwinter.

"I DON'T THINK it's possible to have a perfect garden in all seasons. If I did, what would be the point of carrying on? I guess if I had a perfect spot in my garden, in whatever season it happened to be, if there were seven plants, all of them would be happy and four of them would be performing, doing their thing.

"Looking out the window right now, in midwinter, it's not perfect, but I like looking at the variegated boxwood and the camellia 'Yuletide' because it has that big boss of golden stamens which picks up the yellow on the boxwood. Then, a bit to the right, I like the background of red witch hazel and olearia, and the phormium in the foreground, with its broad, arching, evergreen leaves. It's not perfect, but if I keep my vision really narrow, there's good structure and enough of the elements I like to make it seasonally appealing."

In April, taking the reverse angle—from outside looking in—Kathy again saw something approaching perfection.

"Right now, I like this arrangement, with the boxwood and the ferns, the hellebores and the variegated hakonechloa grass below, and the decrepit little trough, which started out as an alpine trough and is now overflowing with whatever will grow there. That's what I like. I like the fact that the boxwood is a substantial round, forming a point around which everything else can orbit. The fern is very large, but it's soft, so it works with the harder lines of the boxwood. And I like the fact that the boxwood is variegated, which helps to brighten up this dark corner. I like the yellows, in the baby's tears spilling out of the trough and the variegated grass beneath the boxwood. I like the whole effect, because it seems controlled, without being uptight."

Boxwood and baby's tears.

This is an example of Kathy's talent for defining in precise terms *exactly* why a part of her garden is working to her satisfaction, or not. She parses the composition with a well-educated eye. Her education as a gardener began before she learned to read and write.

"I was lucky enough to grow up in Maple Ridge, with a grandfather who lived next door and had studied horticulture at [what is now] the University of Guelph. He really enjoyed plants and had a great big ratty old falling-down greenhouse—the glass was still intact. I watched him sowing seeds with perfectly sifted soil in wooden flats he'd made, growing the flowers that my grandmother loved. As long as I didn't say too much, or knock anything over, I was allowed to sit there and absorb it. As a child, it was somehow comforting.

"My parents loved gardening too. They had a great big garden. I loved to play in it and pick raspberries and strawberries and admire the flowers. If I was really interested and really careful, I'd be allowed to help prick out seedlings in the greenhouse.

"I remember my father got mumps and my mother was looking for something to keep him interested while he was bedridden. So she got him a copy of John Grant's book *Trees and Shrubs for Pacific Northwest Gardens: What to grow and how to grow them*. Well, it may not sound like very diverting reading for the sick, but it really fired a passion for rhododendrons, and they immediately joined the Rhododendron Society. As a child, sleeping on a cold, snowy night wasn't very cozy because the sheets were taken off my bed to cover up the plants that needed protection. My father kept copious notes. I still have his record of a very harsh winter in the 1950s, when all his ceanothus shrubs died, despite the bedsheets."

Kathy has also kept her father's copy of John Grant's book, although it had limited application when she left the west coast with David, her husband, for a new home and her first garden in Port Credit, about twenty-five miles west of Toronto. Their property was small but, having once been lake bottom, endowed with fertile, rich, rock-free loam.

"Everything just shot out of the ground," remembers Kathy. "The previous owners had put in a variety of bulbs. There was scilla and lots of bloodroot and the woods in spring were full of trilliums. Also, my mother started sending me azaleas, but sadly they didn't make it over the winter in Zone 5b."

In Port Credit, while raising her children, Kathy grabbed any opportunity to further her education as a gardener.

"I got to know Leslie Hancock of Woodland Nurseries on Mississauga Road, which was close by, so it was possible to drop the children off at nursery school and then go there. He was a veteran of the Great War and got a land grant, which he used to start his business. By the time I met him he had the best collection of rhododendrons in all of Southern Ontario. So, I used to hang around and talk with him and of course I bought plants.

"Mr. Hancock liked to try new things. He would try all kinds of species, such as *Rhododendron fortunei*, and he experimented with creating new hybrids. He also corresponded with Captain Steele, the famous Nova Scotia rhododendron specialist. I found all this interaction simply fascinating.

"Mr. Hancock was a very important mentor in my early development as a gardener. He was very generous in sharing his experience and knowledge, and very kind to this young woman who probably got in his way when he was trying to get the job done."

And surely, the old man felt equally rewarded by his acquaintance with that young gardener who was so eager to learn from him and became his protégée.

"I became very specific about what I wanted by way of plants. My mother gave me John Grant's book on landscaping, *Garden Design Illustrated* [co-written with Carol L. Grant], which talks about the textures of various plants and how to use them. For instance, you might set a number of small-leaved rhododendrons against a background of a single big-leaved species, and perhaps intermediate sizes in between. So that book was a source of inspiration for me. I still have it and I still follow that principle. Have you read his books? They should be required reading for every gardener. They're so good on how to design a garden so that year-round, it frames your house without overpowering it. It's very west coast."

The writing of Gertrude Jekyll was another source of inspiration for Kathy. Miss Jekyll, a painter, prolific writer, and garden designer, was part of the Arts

The garden frames the house in spring.

and Crafts movement in Britain, early in the twentieth century. Influenced by the Impressionists, she introduced ideas—considered radical at that time—for the use of colour and texture in the garden. She is remembered for her subtle, painterly approach to the arrangement of the gardens she created, particularly for the radiant colour and the brush-like strokes of her plantings. In books such as *Colour Schemes for the Flower Garden*, she originated the concept of using "warm" and "cool" flower colours in gardens.

"I was *very* interested in Gertrude Jekyll's writing. The library in Port Credit was very helpful; they even got me a book that was actually signed by Miss Jekyll. She inspired me. For example, at the end of her borders she would plant a yucca—like a mark of exclamation! It made a really powerful statement. I took that idea. Above all, she made me think a lot about colour. She was very specific about blues—purple blues versus more greeny blues—and what she felt should be woven together and what should be separated; she used cream to break up her hardy plant borders and planted that whole progression from the yellows into the orange, into the red, into the crimson, into the purple, and so on. Which of course I could never do, not having hundred-and-fifty-foot borders and slaves! But she made me *think*. And she wrote beautifully. So, as a source of ideas, books were very important to me, rather than other people's gardens. You see, my neighbours in Port Credit grew nothing but geraniums and roses and bedding plants such as impatiens."

Kathy has had no formal education in landscape design. However, while living and gardening in Port Credit, she took courses in Toronto with the English garden designer, writer, and teacher John Brookes, known for creating gardens that relate to their environment and fit into the wider landscape.

"He's based in England and started out as a surveyor before he got into garden design. He was certainly one of the most influential people in the field in the late twentieth century and he's still at it in his late seventies. He's very exacting and disciplined in the way he sees a design developing for a garden. He likes to take the lines of the house and pull them out into the garden. He uses a lot of geometry, as opposed to 'anything goes.' And for me, it was very good to take his course, because before that, I was very plant focussed, and he certainly made it clear that less is more. You don't need ninety-nine plants. You may need twenty plants, and that's good. He made me think of the effect as a whole, rather than the individual plants. It's quite empowering to read his book and follow his philosophy, because it eliminates a lot of doubt. What he says works. He was certainly a source of inspiration for me. He was a very *demanding* teacher. He scared the wits out of me."

Some twenty years later, with the intervening experience of taking over two gardens in West Vancouver—as much as possible remaking them in her own fashion—all these sources of inspiration, amounting to decades of immersion in the art of gardening, stirred with her own judgment, are poured into her garden on Bowen Island.

"I've been really lucky. There aren't many people who have a chance to build a garden from scratch. And I think I was lucky in that I came to that particular opportunity later in life, after earlier experimenting with three other pieces of property that other people had developed, and trying to make those gardens feel like mine. You learn a lot by doing that. But to come to a virgin site and to be able to build a garden, that is the best of all. That is a huge gift. In 1995, when I first saw this land, it was a bit scary, but I thought it would be just perfect."

From the road, Kathy saw a sunny, southwest-facing slope sweeping down to the sea, with a hundred feet of waterfront: in all nearly an acre for house and garden.

"Never before had we started with raw land, where I could do exactly as I wished to do—including building a house, a small house just for two, along with the garden. So, as John Brookes had taught, I had to think about the context. How is it going to work in the natural landscape? So I actually sweated quite hard over it, to tell you the truth.

"The first decision was prompted by David, who said he didn't want to mow any grass. So there's no lawn, never has been. Instead, I brought in a lot of gravel for pathways and open areas, which of course is really good here because it acts as mulch and helps to hold the water when it rains really hard.

"I had a plan for the basics: the framework of deciduous trees to be planted along the border with our neighbour, the stone wall, the boxwood, the pathways. For a start, I moved some rhododendrons from the West Vancouver garden, but unfortunately a number of them didn't like that. I lost quite a few and I knew that was telling me something about the conditions here. We're on a steep, sunny slope and in summer it can get quite hot and dry. So then I set my sights on plants from New Zealand, which I adore—mainly evergreen shrubs which can take drought, such as olearia, pittosporum, and brachyglottis, as well as perennials such as libertia and pheasant grass. Also, perennial daisies from South Africa, such as osteospermum. And of course, evergreens from California which survive here—the bush anemone, *Carpenteria californica*, various cultivars of small-leaved arctostaphylos, commonly known as bearberry or manzanita, and the prostrate *Ceanothus* 'Point Reyes'.

"A lot of my choices were influenced by reference to Beth Chatto's book *The Dry Garden*. However, I soon learned that a dry garden like hers, set in a field without any root competition, is different from a dry garden here, with Douglas firs. Oh yes!

Maintaining the view in front, with rounded forms and deer-proof, easy-care, drought-resistant plants. PHOTO KATHY LEISHMAN

"In the front, I wanted to maintain the view. I wanted it to be planted with things not on the deer menu—there are so many on this island—and I wanted it to require little or no water during the summer. In order to do that, the choice of plants was pretty narrow. As well as deer-proof, they had to be drought-tolerant. So that meant rosemary, oreganos, and sages; teucrium, santolinas, euphorbias, ozothamnus from New Zealand, and potentilla, which some people sneer at, but in fact I rather like for the warm cinnamony bark in winter. Besides, it blooms endlessly all summer. Cistus. I *love* cistus, though sad to say, the deer have started to nibble them. In imagining the front here, I saw groups of rounded shrubs, rather than pointy-uppy shrubs, giving stability, and I saw lots of grasses in between, because their movement in the wind is lovely. I wanted to make it flow down to the steps, with nothing standing out and demanding attention, so it would all just meld together and you wouldn't be looking at anything *powerful*, just a flow of rounded shapes. The biggest problem is you end up with too many small leaves—not enough foliage with structure.

"And I thought 'easy-care,' because I don't want to be walking down to the beach thinking, 'Oh my God, I really must do whatever, whatever.' I just want

With rounded boxwoods, the garden takes on an air of formality.

to walk down to the beach with my wine and feel happy and have it smell good. It's a hot slope on sunny days, so you get diffusion in the air from the aromatic oils from the lavender and the cistus and the pine. It's quite heady. It looks its best in September when the grasses ripen.

"I THINK GARDENING is one of the few forms of individual expression that is really good for the soul. I really feel that very strongly. When you garden, I think you nurture yourself and, I hope, your family, your children and grandchildren, your neighbours too. It helps us understand where we fit into the environment. It makes us understand that we're all *rooted* on this Earth. We have to connect to where we're from. People think they can get it just by reading a book, but to embrace gardening fully, you have to know the disappointments and the successes—the freezes, the rain, the drought. You have to *do* it, you have to *feel* it."

Yes, to a masterful degree, Kathy does it, and feels it. Into the garden above the house, where a fence, largely obscured by shrubbery, keeps out the deer, she has poured her heart and created a woodland composition of plants that are often rare, sometimes quite ordinary, but always subtly integrated. The perfect plant in the perfect place.

Close to the house, there's an air of formality, expressed in the clipped hedge, the unpainted wooden bench, the stone wall, and the orbs of boxwood. But for the most part, Kathy's taste and flair are joyfully expressed in scenes of *controlled abandon*. She is fearless in her enthusiasm for serendipity, and particularly bold in her willingness to give nature its head. In the month of May, Kathy showed us around again.

"So, right now, I'm seeing *exuberance*. You can tell I like wildness, because what really makes my heart sing is when it's all doing it together. Like here. It's all tied together by the grasses. These are mostly quite ordinary woodland plants, such as the native bleeding heart, *Dicentra formosa*, and that little blue Siberian bugloss, *Brunnera macrophylla* 'Langtrees', along with white and yellow wood anemones and fresh, yellow fern leaves. It's a scene of organized chaos, with plants more or less doing their own thing. I love the fact that they're all doing it together, and all I have to do is weed out the odd bit. I know it looks very loose, but if you don't have lots and lots of time, it's a great way to garden."

Exuberance.

From left to right: *Tulipa* 'Ballerina', *Tulipa batalinii*, *Paeonia mlokosewitschii*. INSET PHOTO KATHY LEISHMAN

Among the ground covers, Kathy includes plants that many gardeners might shun as too invasive, such as wild strawberries, sweet woodruff, the Labrador violet.

"I think, in all honesty, they've incorporated themselves. There are a lot of things that make themselves at home. I've got a big space here and I need colonizers. They do sometimes get out of hand. I've started to pull up some of this Oregon oxalis, because it throttles a lot of other plants. But you know, people love it. It follows the contours of the ground like a blanket. They love the green and the purple underside to the leaf. There's something calm about the way it holds its leaves up."

Inspired by Gertrude Jekyll's use of colour, Kathy's palette in the garden is, once again, loose, apparently unplanned, yet very carefully managed.

"I like all colours. I know some people hate yellow, but how can you hate a sunflower? Or a daffodil? I like yellow, especially in spring, and in autumn too. I like orange. I like the orange of *Tulipa sprengeri*, for instance. With orange, I like brownish or purple foliage. So I have an orangey-beige bed over against the fence, and I have a pastel bed.

"Not everybody likes orange, but right now, I think this really works. I like the orange tulips in this bed, especially the tall 'Ballerina', with the black foliage of the *Anthriscus* 'Ravenswing' and the purple foliage of lysimachia. I like the orange gently repeated in the wallflower below, hiding among the purply-brown leaves of the coral bells. And I love the yellow grass, because it ties everything together. It's *Millium effusum* 'Aureum'. It seeds itself and it pops up here and there, arranging itself and filling in the gaps. It's gentle and

it's not thuggish. It's a very good grass. If ever you want some, I'll bring you some. Would you like some?

"Here's a softer colour grouping. The little peach-coloured tulip is a species, *Tulipa batalinii*. I like the fact that the iris leaves are glaucous green and the petals of the tulip are peachy coloured with just a hint of green, so it's not such a dramatic contrast. Then when the iris opens, it's the same colour as the tulip. Some years they do it together, and some years they don't. When they do, it's a good moment—but not this year.

"Here is the peony Molly the witch. It's a species and the nickname comes from its proper botanical name, which is *Paeonia mlokosewitschii*. Quite a mouthful! I like the foliage and the simple, single-petal, yellow flowers. It's the only yellow herbaceous peony. Again, at this time of year, this mix really works for me.

"I need the silver lunaria background here, because the disporum is so dark. This is one of Dan Hinkley's introductions from the wild. He called it 'Night Heron'. It's amazing, almost black. Here again I like the fact that this area is all quite wild. I like to pick a plant, find the right spot, and just let it rip. I guess the only problem is that sometimes it's so happy with its spot that it produces tons of seedlings, which I don't always want!"

Kathy's observations are detailed.

"That crinodendron is going to bloom within the next few weeks. It's just above the rhododendron there. It will be loaded with flowers. It's quite artificial-looking, because the bells are so intense in their colour and the shape is so particular."

She is her own fiercest critic.

To Kathy's eye, this area needs re-designing.

"Now this little bit of garden I need to work on. There's something wrong. I think what happened is we made a new path and we didn't rework the other side. So I need something with a little more physical presence, just past that white tulip. If you look at it from here you can see it needs something with impact. But I haven't found the perfect plant yet. I suppose I could go with a nice little dome of dwarf berberis.

"THERE'S TREMENDOUS JOY in gardening, I think, and a tremendous amount of sharing. Generosity is huge among gardeners. They're always ready to share a tip, or a cutting, or whatever they've got. I find gardeners are usually pretty wide-ranging in their other interests. They're often interested in music or art. They tend to have inquiring and open minds. I feel we shouldn't judge a garden just because we might not have chosen the same plants. People can do anything they want, and provided they do it well, that deserves respect and admiration. If people want to have rows of marigolds, well, why not? I like the smell.

"I've felt the pain of leaving a garden behind and moving on. Leaving Port Credit wasn't a problem. It was a pretty garden and I loved my relationship

Kathy, her delightfully cluttered greenhouse, and an ornamental kale in flower.

with it, but we were moving to a better climate. Leaving our first garden in West Vancouver was a little harder, but I was moving to a larger garden with huge possibilities. I was over the moon. Leaving *that* garden was a terrible wrench, because it was a *very* good site. But I've come to realize that a garden is a transitory thing. You try to create a work of art. You have your fun. When you leave, you take your memories with you. You don't have to worry about what happens five years down the line, or ten. What other people do with it is their business.

"I suppose there will come a time when I have to give up this place, but as a way of making it easier and easier, I'm letting every arbutus seedling be. I'm letting nature take its course. I'm letting all the shrubbery grow that fits with that aesthetic, and by God, if that's all I have left, that's just fine. What could be more beautiful?"

Fremontodendron californicum.

TWO

Windcliff

THIS STORY COULD BEGIN WITH "Once upon a time . . ." For it is the story of an enchanted garden and a gardener who conjures life from the wild-collected seeds of rare and difficult plants.

His website is headed "Daniel J. Hinkley, plantsman."

That is a title of distinction, not to be assumed lightly. It implies a very wide knowledge of plants, their habitats and habits, together with field experience on different continents, studying, collecting, and photographing plants in the wild. A plantsman's second language is botanical Latin. The plantsman has experience and skill in propagation and cultivation. He (or she—the term is applied equally to women) knows the right place for the right plant, yet is adventurous in trying new ideas. He has a good eye for the aesthetics of gardening: the balance of structure, the harmonious blending of texture in leaf and bark, the knowing use of colour.

The plantsman loves plants. Indeed, is probably *obsessed.*

Dan Hinkley is a plantsman of the first rank, one of just three Americans recognized as such in the online encyclopedia Wikipedia. In addition, he is an author, lecturer, and teacher.

The enchanted garden is Windcliff, a name that precisely describes the setting: a high bluff on the shore of Puget Sound, near Indianola in Washington State. On a clear day, there's a distant view of Mount Rainier, dominating the horizon to the southeast.

Dan Hinkley, plantsman.

The mountain was lost in mist when we visited Windcliff on a lightly overcast day in late spring.

Even the approach is enchanting. After navigating the winding roads of the Kitsap Peninsula, we drove for about a kilometre up a narrow, private lane, bordered by a second-growth woodland canopy of cedars, maples with limbs draped in moss and licorice ferns, and an understorey of sword ferns and huckleberries.

At Windcliff, we were warmly and wetly greeted by Max and Odie, Dan's boisterous American springer spaniels. They have the run of the place and, inside, sleep in luxury in big baskets by the Aga stove.

TRULY, IT SEEMS that Dan was born to be a plantsman.

"I've had a fascination with seeds, ever since I was four or five years old. I would take them and put them in pots on the windowsill—orange pips and avocados. Those are some of my earliest memories. I don't know where that came from. My parents certainly weren't gardeners, but they didn't discourage me. My mom formed an Audubon society, and strongly encouraged us kids to be aware of the natural world. And living in a rural situation in northern Michigan, prior to the time when kids were meant to fear the wild, we were urged to get out of the house and go for a walk in the woods and fields. What a different world it is now!

"I've had a vegetable garden since I was seven. My dad was a farmer, and then he became a pharmacist, and had to work seven days a week. So I tended the vegetable garden. I loved doing that. I *still* love doing that. Nothing can beat veg, fresh from the garden. It's so rewarding. Robert and I eat from this garden all year round.

The vegetable garden at Windcliff.

"We don't eat a lot of potatoes, but I do like to grow different varieties. Right now I have nine. One of them is 'Ozette'. It came up the coast from Peru with the Spanish and was given to the Makah Indian tribes, whose territory is in this area. They had it going for well over two hundred years. So it's a hand-me-down potato, a very interesting, corky-skinned, fingerling type."

Vegetables are grown in raised beds and enormous clay pots, which well serve the function of food production. But it's much more than that. Like many other installations at Windcliff, both inside the house and out, this food garden is itself a work of art, full of fun and pleasing to the eye. The layout suggests a courtyard, floored with paving stones and beach pebbles. The raised beds form the perimeter and the huge pots stand in line down the middle. At the far end, three wonderfully zany, intricate iron works are hung in a gallery. Cut from steel plate with a welding torch, these are the creations of Mark Bulwinkle, a California sculptor.

"I ALWAYS KNEW that working with plants was what I was going to do. To be honest, I think my parents were absolutely astounded that I made a living, because I saw the glances they were shooting each other. 'Going into horticulture! He's not going to make any money doing that.'"

Nevertheless, Dan plunged into the plant kingdom, first earning a BSc in horticulture from Michigan State University, then later a master's in urban horticulture at the University of Washington. That led to a position as instructor of horticulture at Edmonds Community College, on the outskirts of Seattle, where he taught for ten years. From Edmonds, a ferry crosses Puget Sound to Kingston, in Kitsap County. There, in 1987, with his partner, Robert Jones, an architect, Dan bought land and developed the garden and the nursery for which he became famous: Heronswood.

Like many nurseries, Heronswood started as an offshoot of building a big garden. From propagation and division, there are plenty of extra plants. Why not sell them? To begin with, one Thanksgiving Day, Dan and Robert assembled a fifty-foot hoop house—a simple sort of greenhouse with a plastic roof stretched over flexible piping. The nursery operated out of that for the first four years.

"That's where we produced everything, and we never, ever imagined it getting to be as big a business as it eventually became."

Heronswood became a big business because it was no ordinary nursery; it was no ordinary nursery because it was stocked with plants that Dan grew from seed he had collected in the wild, on six continents.

In the days of the great plant hunters a hundred years ago and more, it was quite usual for nurseries and seedsmen to fund the travels of plant collectors, who would then of course turn over the seed to their patrons. In this case, Dan was both collector and nurseryman. He raised funds for his explorations by selling shares. Then, upon returning home, he sent shareholders a complete list of the seed collected, and they chose thirty packets.

"It was a lot, *a lot*, of work—and by the time I'd cleaned and divided up all those seeds, I would've been just as well off having a bake sale! Eventually, the nursery grew to the point where it was funding my travels. I can't say that the plants themselves brought in much income, but the mystique of a plant hunter's nursery was certainly good for business."

In becoming a plant hunter, Dan acknowledges the inspiration of two more senior plantsmen.

"J.C. Raulston, at North Carolina State University, certainly sparked that ambition. He really was the founder of the new plant frontier in the US, and it was his embrace of the whole diversity of plants that helped ignite my own passion. I already had the nursery when I got to know him. He would come and visit and we'd exchange plants.

"He was a special spirit, with a degree of generosity that very few people I've ever met possess. He meant so much to me that I try to pass that generosity on, in one way or another. When I get emails from people saying, 'You don't know me, but I've got this question . . . ,' I remember his example, and rather than just deleting it, I think of J.C. and the fact that he would have answered it. He never talked down to people.[1]

"The English plantsman Roy Lancaster also inspired me, because his writing covers everything—I mean the entire tree of life, not just plants. So, like him, when I travel I'm asking 'What's that bird and what is it eating?' and 'What's that they're selling in the market?'"

Dan's first plant-hunting trip was in Korea. He travelled on his own and, quite by chance, met fellow plant explorers, Bleddyn and Sue Wynn-Jones of Crûg Farm Nursery in North Wales. The three became good friends and have travelled together several times since.

"From that beginning, things just *meshed* for me, and the process of collecting, recording, verifying, propagating, and offering just built upon itself very quickly. It all seemed to make perfect sense. But I can't remember ever sitting down and saying to myself, 'I'm going to start a nursery based on collecting material in the wild.'"

In collecting, Dan's ideal habitat has been in areas just on the edge of hardiness, generally broadleaf forests bordering on the subtropical. He has always wanted to introduce plants that had a good chance of flourishing in the Pacific Northwest. Such plants would sustain the nursery, but he also acknowledges that he has had his own garden in mind.

"Not that I wouldn't be very interested in exploring tropical areas, but when the plant life had no application to these parts, I really couldn't justify it."

Beesia deltophylla. PHOTO DAN HINKLEY

There are plants in gardens today that Dan Hinkley collected in the wild, grew from seed at Heronswood, and introduced to a market of discriminating gardeners always on the lookout for something new. "A surprising number," says Dan, although, with typical modesty, he's never made a list.

For example, he introduced *Beesia deltophylla*, a ground cover with shiny, heart-shaped leaves, which has become very popular in temperate areas of North America. There's *Disporum cantoniense* 'Night Heron', an almost-black-leaved variation that Dan collected in China, then propagated and named. In Sichuan Province he found another disporum, which he called 'Green Giant'. He has introduced hardy scheffleras.

"There are others. I don't dwell on it all that much, although it is sort of quietly fulfilling when you think that a number of plants had not been secured in cultivation until I collected them. I tend to think that my forte as a nurseryman has been popularizing plants, rather than having actually introduced them.

"On the other hand, I'm not willing to describe plants I've collected as 'discoveries.' They may seem new to cultivation, but you can't *really* know what has been in this country before, or in Europe. And secondly, when you say, 'I discovered this plant,' you're discounting the fact that the native people have been using that plant for ten thousand years in their culture."

In his honour, somebody named a Chinese mahonia that Dan collected *Mahonia fortunei* 'Dan Hinkley'. In the field of botanical nomenclature, it is unthinkable that a collector would name a plant for himself; that recognition must be bestowed by others.

"I would *shudder* to think that I would ever consider doing that."

By the mid-1990s, Heronswood Nursery was doing a thriving mail-order business, and the display garden tours attracted international interest. Dan was also well known as a hybridizer, breeding new, choice cultivars, particularly hellebores. We remember joining a busload of fellow hardy-plant enthusiasts, leaving Vancouver very early one frosty February morning. Our destination was Heronswood, and our purpose to choose from one of the finest selections of hellebores on the west coast. The bus parked at the nursery gate, some distance from the greenhouses, and we (usually) well-mannered, mostly elderly gardeners shoved (without appearing to shove) and rushed (without appearing to rush), hell-bent on being first to grab the blackest blacks, yellowest yellows, and reddest reds. It was a feeding frenzy. The best were sold in seconds.

In 2000, Dan and Robert sold Heronswood to Burpee Seeds but continued to run the nursery until May 2006, when George Ball, the company president, abruptly closed it.

"We obviously wouldn't have sold the place if we weren't ready to move on. But what we found troubling was the lack of grace with which it was closed, not the fact that it was closed. It seemed such a waste. I thought it would soon be bulldozed and built over, but nothing happened for years. I'd much

rather see a garden die quickly, be euthanized, than to suffer neglect and decay. It's just a plant collection. Nothing more. I have absolutely no sentimentality about leaving a garden.[2]

"Also, to be frank, one of the reasons I feel somewhat grateful we don't have Heronswood anymore is that a lot of the things we considered real rarities you find now at the local supermarket. With tissue culture, the competition to offer something that's truly new and unusual is steep. When we were at Heronswood, we felt the pressure every year to offer something distinctive, but now, what is rare and distinctive one day is common fare the next. The variety of plants offered by nurseries seems to have plummeted in the last five years. It's pretty dismal out there."

Schefflera alpina.

SERENDIPITY SEEMS TO play a part in the lives of many gardeners, and it was serendipity, at least in part, that brought Dan and Robert to Windcliff.

"This property was owned by two women who'd lived here for fifty years and they loved gardening. We had visited one time, and the thing that stuck in my mind was the amount of lawn they had, and the staggering view. But, most important, I knew in my heart of hearts that we would *never* be able to afford a place like this. It was beyond belief. Then, when we knew we were going to sell Heronswood, we wrote them a letter saying we were looking for a new property. We liked the area. They knew it well. If they happened to hear of anything becoming available, would they please let us know? And they called us the very day they got the letter and said, 'We would really love it if you would consider taking *our* property!' I guess they wanted us to take it on because they knew we would preserve it. There wasn't even any negotiation. We signed the papers within a week. They've both passed away now, but I think they would approve of what we've done. I hope so."

THE EXPLORER'S GARDEN is the title of two of Dan Hinkley's books. One is subtitled *Rare and Unusual Perennials*, the other *Shrubs and Vines from the Four Corners of the World*. Both present plants he has found and photographed in the wild, describe the qualities they contribute to the garden, and provide advice on propagation and cultivation. Windcliff is the explorer's garden in the making.

"Ultimately, my aim is to have all plants here of wild origin—that's to say, grown from seed I've collected in the wild. I'm not a purist in that regard, and I've put in other plants that work for me here. But when push comes to shove, when a new plant goes in, one I didn't collect is going to go out."

Dan first showed us some of his treasures that surround the house.

Scheffleras are usually found as ornamental, evergreen, indoor plants, suffering in silence as they gather dust in the corner of an office. Dan, however, has collected and propagated several species that will survive *outdoors*, in sheltered gardens of the Pacific Northwest.

"That holboellia happens to be quite beautiful. It's a Vietnamese species, a quite extraordinary vine that's not known at all. It really is pretty in there, entwined among the berberis.

Holboellia brachyantha.

"Pure serendipity."

"The clematis was already here. I planted round it, and there are times when it grows right up into the trachycarpus when it's in bloom, and they're truly beautiful together. It's pure serendipity."

There was a flash of orange and black—the first black-headed grosbeak of the year. Dan pointed out a bald eagle in its massive, twiggy nest, high in an old-growth Douglas fir.

"You can just see its head. Obviously it's keeping its chicks warm."

In an enclave on the sheltered side of the house, there's a brilliant mingling of ceramic bamboo with Chinese fairy bells (*Disporum cantoniense* 'Green Giant'), collected by Dan in Sichuan and subsequently introduced

The Chusan palm (*Trachycarpus fortunei*).

Disporum cantoniense 'Green Giant', in Marcia Donahue's bamboo grove.

at Heronswood. Both are rooted in the plush greenery of beesia, grasses, and ferns. The ceramics are the work of Marcia Donahue, a potter and gardener who combines the two in her famous garden in Berkeley, California. She makes the bamboo in tubes of varied length, each one of a kind, glazed in earthy hues, then threaded on rebar. Dan told us she used to do mammoth stonework, but is now working with clay and creating, among other works, these bamboo groves.

"She made these specifically for this site. She calls them *Bambusa sinensis* var. *maritima*!"

We rounded the corner to the front of the house, where the air is full of sweet harmony: birdsong, trickling water, and a ribbit-ribbiting chorus of frogs.

"I've always liked wet gardens, so we created this tiny bog. It's mainly to encourage the bird life. And the frogs, singing in the springtime. There are tree frogs and leopard frogs. I love the sound of them. And it's a sign of a pretty healthy ecosystem. Just look at the number of tadpoles. Of course, I didn't reckon on Max and Odie loving it too. They play in here and get covered in mud.

"That's one of Marcia's pillows, and the head is hers too—well no, not literally!"

After the house was renovated and additions built, Dan and Robert made a plan for the patio, with the intent of bringing the water up, literally and metaphorically—pulling Puget Sound closer to the house, as it were. Next to the patio, they put in rills and pools, creating the sound of water and the sight of water reflected on water, giving the illusion of being much closer to the beach. There used to be fish too, lots of them, until one summer evening when three British Columbia gardeners drove down the coast to visit Dan.

A head and a pillow: ceramics by Marcia Donahue.

"I remember Kathy Leishman, Pam Frost, and Beverley Merryfield were here one time. We had a lovely evening and sat out watching our gorgeous koi and goldfish, and Kathy said, 'Haven't you ever had otters?' and I said, 'No, thankfully not.' That night, *that night*, was when the otters came. It was almost as if they'd called them forth. The fish were completely wiped out over three nights. The creatures come back periodically to see if we've been kind enough to restock, but no, I'm not raising fish to feed hungry otters. To be honest with you, it was quite painful. I'd become quite attached to those fish—and they were just massacred."

Dan credits two sources of inspiration for the garden at Windcliff.

"One is the movie *Enchanted April*, which I saw about twenty years ago. It's set on the northwest coast of Italy, where four Englishwomen rent an old hilltop castle for the month. Two have wormy husbands. They're all unhappy and the castle garden seems to bring them back to life. It always struck me as a wonderful garden. It's not fussy. It's very Mediterranean. I've gone back and watched the movie several times, and I still feel right about it. It was the type of garden everybody had to explore on their own; they discovered their own personal places and found their own moments. The movie wasn't about

a garden at all. But in some ways it was, because it was the garden that brought everybody together and provided a setting for them to rediscover contentment.

"The other is the late film director Derek Jarman's garden.[3] I saw it for the first time in the late 1980s and I've been back since. It's nothing like this. It's a dry, hot, bleak, treeless, windswept patch of stony land opposite a nuclear power plant, right on the southern coast of England. It's a remarkable embrace of the site. Like his movies, it's very, very original. I mean, who would have thought of using a nuclear power plant as the borrowed scenery?"

Inspired by these gardens, Dan set out to evoke a Mediterranean feeling in front of the house. Knowing this was a hot, dry, relatively lifeless bluff, he planted hundreds of plants in tiny plugs, all of which he had propagated with this site in mind. For three consecutive years, he marched across the bluff, three hundred and thirty feet in all, planting one section after another and then, in the fourth year, suturing it all together with the terrace. Much of this was experimental, because he couldn't be certain which plants would thrive in the wind and salt spray, in full sun.

Enchanted Windcliff, somewhat inspired by the movie *Enchanted April*.

"Even now, I see some things that don't quite fit. I mean, it doesn't make any sense to have that weeping styrax there, but on the other hand, when it comes out in spring with that lovely, saucy foliage, I love it. So there's no

Grasses meant "to be looked *through*, not *at*."

question I can develop some affection for a plant, but then again—catch me on the wrong day and no plant is safe!"

We stayed well back from the edge of the bluff. It's very unstable.

"I'm afraid there are some very raw, young areas in front here, but I'm well past the stage of thinking that my garden can't change. The winter sorted this area out two years ago. It was a brutal winter, and I hacked and hacked dead plants away. Even the arbutus trees, out there on the edge of the bluff, were horribly damaged. But now that it's happened, I'm creating these new corridors. I'm planting grasses. I was never a big proponent of grasses—certainly not at Heronswood, but in retrospect that was not a grass garden. Grasses are meant to be looked *through*, not *at*. And this is a good place to look through them toward the light off the sea, to catch that diaphanous quality, and to watch what the wind does, providing that sense of motion in a garden that I find so enchanting.

"My practice is to plant grasses *singly*, rather than in big clumps, which has been the North American landscape fad: huge stands of one grass and then sedum and then something else. But when you plant them in groups, you don't see the plant; you just see a solid mass, a wall."

FEW GARDENERS GROW plants from seed, other than vegetables and annuals. Very few try to grow *all* they need from seed. However, fulfillment of

The dove, or handkerchief, tree (*Davidia involucrata*).

Dan's ambition at Windcliff depends upon his wholehearted commitment to growing his own.

"I find the process utterly fascinating—all that information contained in such a neat little packet, the seed. How the pollination happens, how the distribution of seed happens—it's a small world of wonders.

"Also, the resulting variation is so interesting. As you talk to gardeners, it becomes very apparent that most *think* they know a plant. They know a plant because they have one individual of that species. But once you start growing from seed, you find out there's variation. I think more gardeners should try it. For a start, there are so many plants you can't get except from seed. Sure, it takes patience and a lot of times it doesn't work out. But when it does, the results are interesting and satisfying, and people can take pride in saying, 'I grew that tree, that shrub, that bulb, from seed.' I guess I'm greedy as well: I want lots of one thing and that's the cheapest way to do it!

"Then there are those *aha!* moments in the garden when you're looking for something you put in and you can't find it and you look up and there it is—a tree! That happens much more quickly from seed than most gardeners realize. It's a mistake to believe that there's all that much time between a seed and the shrub in a five-gallon container that most people buy. I've always been a proponent of buying smaller sizes, because the amount of growing time between one and the other is minuscule. Besides which, there's a better chance of a quick takeoff and survival if they're planted out when small."

It's true; even though Dan's garden at Windcliff is only eight years old, it has a well-settled air of maturity, especially among the trees and shrubbery, the arboretum, which fills the larger part of the property.

"The woodland garden at Heronswood was where I found my type of gardening—trying to capture the feel of natural habitat, but using an enormous range of plants. The woodland was already there, an overstorey of conifers mostly. We did create a middle layer, an interesting range of broadleaf evergreen trees as well as dogwoods and so on that seemed to thrive underneath the Doug firs. Then there was a shrub layer and finally the carpet of herbaceous perennials. That's being applied here at Windcliff to the whole site, but we started with very little overstorey. We're building that."

At Windcliff, the woodland garden includes plants of the original garden that Dan chose to leave in place. The davidia was already there. From seed, it can take fifteen years or more to grow a dove tree to blossoming size, and Dan decided that this tree deserved to be an exception to his overall aim of creating the garden from wild-collected seed. Many of the rhododendrons are from the original garden. While Dan would never plant a hybrid rhododendron—generally, only *species* are found in the wild—these were well established and help give a sense of maturity to the garden. At least for the time being, they stay. However, every plant along the driveway began life as wild-collected seed.

"When we moved here from Heronswood, I also took some plants that were *meaningful* to me, especially ones that people had given me over the years. For example, Christopher Lloyd once gave me a fern, and I made sure that came here. Rosemary Verey gave me a boxwood from her garden at Barnsley. That's here. Plants have so many different layers, not just the name and the origin but all the other associations, including memory. Those are two that bring back memories of great gardeners and friends now gone."

As we moved on, Dan occasionally stooped to pull weeds.

"It's the season of annual fireweed. Next the alder comes along. It's like a calendar of weeds. It's always been my thought that weeds are co-evolving with humans to become more and more invasive."

We followed him through his woodland garden as he introduced us to some favourites.

Top: *Helwingia chinensis.*

Above: *Magnolia wilsonii.*

"Here's a remarkable plant I collected in China. It's *Helwingia chinensis*. The flowers are smack dab in the middle of the leaf. The flower stems are fused to the midrib of the leaf. This is a female, so it will form black fruit right on top of the leaf. I have other species where the fruit is red."

The woodland was lit up by the glow of a variegated dogwood, a tree with the airy elegance of a ballet dancer. The tree proclaimed its shining beauty, its branches generously offering gifts of clusters of small white flowers in bud.

"Well, it's quite a dilemma, because this is not from my wild-collected material. But it's so happy, and here I go making all sorts of exceptions to my rule. But I wouldn't be without this tree."

Dan was interrupted by the agitated trilling of a spotted towhee.

"It must have a nest nearby. It's Max. He takes the babies. They don't have a chance because towhees nest on the ground, or close to it. Easy pickings for Max. Much as I love that dog, I hate senseless death. I need to convince him that he's a Buddhist."

Even so, the woodland at Windcliff is filled with birdsong.

"Come and look at the *Magnolia wilsonii*. Most magnolias have up-facing flowers. What I really admire about this species is the drooping flowers. You have to get under to really appreciate it. Absolute perfection. Beautiful fragrance. I also like magnolias that bloom in late spring, so you get the blossom with the young leaves. It makes a lovely contrast.

Cornus controversa variegata.

Sassafras tzumu.
INSET PHOTO
DAN HINKLEY

"Here's a sassafras that I collected in northeast Sichuan eight years ago. It's so beautiful after a shower of rain, like now. You can see the pearly water droplets on the leaves. This bloomed here for the first time last month. As a matter of fact, I was working in my greenhouse and happened to look up, and noticed a distant haze of yellow. It was thrilling to see it. And look at the variation in the shape of the leaves. I was always fond of telling my students that it wore right-hand, left-hand, and mutant-handed mittens!

"It's amazing how the trees I planted have come into their own in our woodland garden. It's ever-evolving of course, becoming more and more woodland-like. And that brings to mind the whole concept of the garden over time. Even if you start with a full-sun garden, if you plant any woodies at all, you end up with a shade garden.

"I guess I would like to get to the point of some sort of *stasis*, where I have included long-term investments. I mean long-living plants that are not overwhelming but which will reduce the amount of maintenance while still providing year-round effect. There are moments when I feel I'm getting closer to that, and then some winter will come along like the one we just had and set me back.

The flower of the *Aristolochia kaempferi*, and Dan Hinkley showing its "one-way-door" mechanism.

"I suppose it's a part of the evolution of the gardener, a spiral staircase where you can never quite see where you're going or where you're going to end up. It's a very personal odyssey. But I think we all end up in the same place, understanding that gardening is about foliage, about texture, about scale, and accepting that flowers are just a little bit of icing on the cake. And I think it's about savouring the moment in the garden, because it comes and goes so quickly.

"In truth, I'm approaching sixty and I have a lot of other interests in life. I take piano lessons. I enjoy reading. I like to ride my bike and go hiking. I don't want to be a one-dimensional gardener. Much as I love it, I don't want to be a slave to it. I don't want to spend all my time just weeding and pruning!"

AS WE SAID goodbye to Dan and his enchanted garden, accepting farewell shloopy kisses from Max and Odie, he spotted another rarity in bloom.

"You *must* look at this. This is a wonderful flower—*Aristolochia kaempferi*, commonly called Dutchman's pipe. It's a vine that I collected in northeast Sichuan, and its fertilization is an incredible story."

Dan picked a flower and pulled it apart to demonstrate.

"It has a one-way-door system. It gives off pheromones, which bring insects in, and then it keeps them there and they try to escape through this ring. It's a false window, like a stained-glass window, so the insects are trying to get out, but they can't. And then, eventually, an insect will come along with pollen and at that point, once fertilization is effected, the anthers in the flower release their pollen, dust all the living insects with it, and then the door opens! It's not warm enough yet to see this wonderful process, but if you hold that up to the light you can see the false window. Isn't that magical? I love showing that to kids."

Vancouver Island across Georgia Strait, viewed from Eva's rocky landscape.

THREE

The Landscape Is Within Me

Eva Diener, painter and gardener.

EVA DIENER THE PAINTER AND Eva Diener the gardener are inextricably bound to the Earth and its landscapes. She's been a noted painter for more than forty years, producing canvases that often display huge, expressionistic images, many inspired by nature. The garden, which she built and shares with her husband, Erwin, grows on British Columbia's Sunshine Coast. Though only metres away from the glorious rocky shores and surf of Georgia Strait, the Diener garden is a hidden, magical place of woodland, dry land, moss-covered rocks, blossoming shrubs, floral treasures, and trees, trees, trees.

The variety of species in this garden gives it the status of a botanical collection, a carefully created and nurtured collection, almost unimaginable in private hands. The garden's genesis has spanned continents as the Dieners moved from Europe to Australia to North America. Their eventual settlement on the BC coast is the joyful culmination of a lifelong love affair with nature.

Eva's intense practical knowledge of plants started in childhood, in the small town of Küsnacht on the outskirts of Zürich, Switzerland.

"The garden and art—I grew up with both, right from the beginning," she says. "I was a late child and my three siblings were older. I was lucky to grow up with a large garden, which was part of my breathing space, my being. And so was the landscape beyond, where so often the whole family would go for long walks. They were all grown-ups and I was like a puppy, running

Descending through woodland to reach the garden.

and jumping beside them. Being close to the ground, I could see the most, better than any of them, except my grandfather. He would talk about the mosses, the lichens, and the tiny fungi. He taught me to train my eyes, to experience the landscape with my whole being. He always carried a magnifying glass and would show me the smallest details, those inconspicuous features that are so often decisive in determining the identity of the plant.

"And, right from the beginning, I observed the different kinds of landscapes: a gully where you have a shadowy side and a sunny side, and accordingly different plants; one kind of geological formation leading to another. Then, emerging from the gully onto a sunny plain, there would be meadow plants, and again, different ones along the paths. This awareness of nature came right at the beginning of my life. Nothing came earlier. I sharpened my eyes right from early childhood. My first memories are of me physically being part of the landscape.

"My growing awareness of nature, and how it works—how geology works, how climate works—this sensibility developed as I also learned to appreciate the aesthetics of the landscapes I loved in Switzerland. Always together—the aesthetics I discovered in nature, the art I learned about in the house. My aunt was one of the early academic women of her time. She taught art history and from her, I discovered painting. I started to draw and paint. It was a natural thing for me to do, as was gardening. As a child, I wanted be an artist; I also wanted to be a botanist, an acrobat. So many choices! But most of all, I wanted to paint."

Eva's garden is off a cul-de-sac on a country road outside Sechelt. The approach to the house, perched upon a magnificent expanse of rock, does not suggest that a large garden is part of the five-acre surroundings. To reach the garden, we made our way down a narrow, switchback path and into woodland alive with infinite foliage and tantalizing touches of colour here and there.

Rhododendron litiense, centre, with *R. sutchuenense* and *R. fortunei discolor* behind.

The path led around and through a forest containing a collection of species rhododendrons interspersed with native conifers. Through a high wooden gate, we entered into an expanse of winding paths and a breathtaking array of plants, trees, and shrubs.

"What is important for me is that the view, from wherever you stand, should be pleasing—at all heights and from all distances. When planning the garden, I realized I was facing a real challenge, because the garden would not relate to a house, as it normally does, nor to an entrance, nor to any big feature such as a pond. There were some beautiful rock outcrops in the land, but there

Entering the garden, with much to discover as yet hidden from view.

was no starting or focus point. So I set myself the task of creating a landscape so that you can stand anywhere in the whole area, you can turn around in a circle, stop, and wherever you look, it has to be *perfect*. By that I mean interesting to the eye in the close, immediate view, the middle, and in the distance. Shrubs and trees of different heights. Some pleasing sights hidden to a certain degree but not altogether, so that everywhere you turn, you sense continuity. Occasionally, I allowed the path to take a sharp angle, so as to change the vista drastically. Above all, the garden should be more than just a collection of plants. Each plant should be selected and placed to fit the flow of its surrounding environment. I plan, wherever possible, to group plants together according to how and where they grow in the wild."

We visited Eva's garden in the middle of a cool Pacific Northwest April. Standing in the main, original area of her expansive garden, Eva surveyed the array of trees, some distant on the perimeter, others close by. Most, after twenty years, have reached mature height.

In her soft, pleasantly accented voice, her botanical Latin positively purrs as she names her trees. "Looking north, the tallest is *Nothofagus obliqua*, which,

like the nearby stands of the southern beech, *N. antarctica*, and the evergreen *N. dombeyi*, is native to Patagonia. It's deciduous, the loosely growing crown contrasting with the denser katsura (*Cercidiphyllum japonicum*). To the left are the naked branches of *Alangium platanifolium*, a medium-sized tree which leafs out very late in spring. The *Stewartia pseudocamellia* was one of our half-dozen extravagances. It was already a mature tree when we bought it, while all the others were two or three feet tall at the most. It bears single, white blooms in July.

Foreground, left to right: *Styrax obassia, Acer palmatum* 'Sango Kaku', *Stewartia pseudocamellia.*

"In front, just leafing out, is the lighter-coloured green *Styrax obassia*. You can still see the fruit of the *Styrax japonica*. Also, an old sour cherry tree, now in blossom, which doesn't have enough sun in this climate. Although it's sick, it still grows fruit—but the raccoons don't share any with us! Every year we think it should go, but then it blossoms and we love it and so we keep it."

Magnolia 'Caerhays Belle'.

Franklinia alatamaha, *Asimina triloba*, *Asimina parviflora* (both are species of pawpaw tree), *Albizia julibrissin* (the Persian silk tree)—garden rarities all. Eva remembers the melodious names of her trees like dear old friends, a story or painterly description attached to each.

"The most dominant of all these trees, the magnificent *Catalpa speciosa*, flowering in July, is another of our extravagances. We found it languishing in a field outside Vancouver, after it had done its duty of beautifying the Expo '86 grounds. We rescued it."

Eva's magnolia collection in itself is distinguished. She turned this way and that, drawing our attention to evergreen *Magnolia grandiflora*, *M. virginiana* (the sweetbay magnolia), *M. dawsoniana*, *M. sargentiana*, *M. campbellii*, and more.

"I'm excited about the *Magnolia officinalis*. It's one of the tallest—you can just make out its tip over there. The large, slightly greenish-white flowers are in harmony with the extremely large leaves, similar to my even more beloved *Magnolia hypoleuca*, the whitebark magnolia. Then, I especially love the hybrid *Magnolia* 'Woodsman'—its flowers combining olive green and various subdued shades of Bordeaux, rose, and violet. Into it grows a deep-violet clematis.

Clerodendrum trichotomum.

"Underneath the tall leafy trees, we have *Clerodendrum trichotomum*, commonly called harlequin glorybower, which flowers, so sweetly scented, in August. Some of the other trees are different varieties of sorbus, known as mountain ash or rowan. There's a *Phellodendron amurense*, the Amur cork tree, and the tall one is *Fraxinus angustifolia*, an ash, and over there is the climbing hydrangea, creating a romantic, leafy bower around the little fountain. Perhaps you can hear the gentle splashing."

Flowing through this arboretum, bordering the narrow pathways, is a riotous carpet of woodland ground covers. There are ferns, fritillaries, and fawn lilies, both pink and white, cyclamen and epimediums, hellebores, cranesbill,

Letting nature take its course on the woodland floor. Clockwise from top left: epimediums, pink fawn lilies, cyclamen, fritillaries, hellebores.

Allium 'Globemaster'.

anemones, and mayapple. All mingle in carefree exuberance, spreading and self-seeding, according to nature's whim. In early summer, the balled heads of allium steal the show, in shades of mauve and purple.

Eva's painter's eye is always engaged.

"Always aware. Even when I look at a stack of towels on a shelf, I am conscious of the pleasing arrangement of colour: how the pinks, blues, and purples go together. And I notice how the sun shines through clothes hanging on a hook.

"So every time we walk through this little gate, we give a great sigh of pure pleasure. We marvel at the variations on themes of green, and the different shapes of foliage with just some blossom. Walking through the garden is the same as walking your eyes through a painting. And there's pleasure for the ear, too, because of the birds. This garden is home to a great number of species. I usually carry my binoculars."

But Eva seldom merely walks in the garden. She skips. She strides, sometimes calling out a warning in case of an intruding black bear. Though tiny, elfin, she has great presence. In the studio, her painting style is positively athletic. As she confronts a canvas and starts to apply the paint, it is with sweeping, confident arcs of movement and range of motion. For larger works, she climbs a stepladder. Her beginnings as a painter, however, were on a smaller scale. While at university in Zürich, she met and married Erwin. Eva taught while he finished his PHD.

Walking through Eva's garden delights all the senses.

"We moved to the suburbs of Zürich and into a tiny flat. Luckily, we were surrounded by large trees. I went to evening classes at the art school and in my spare time, I would paint. I had plucked up my courage and bought small pieces of cardboard and small tubes of paint, all the while counting pennies while I used up the paint. I painted the trees and the landscape I saw out of the window."

Their horizons broadened considerably after Erwin obtained a post-doctoral fellowship as an immunologist in Melbourne, Australia. When they found a place to live outside the city, Eva was enchanted.

"It was wonderful—a house we could rent with a lovely front and back garden—so beautiful! You cannot imagine our happiness. Full of trees, foreign plants, Australian plants. It was paradise! Living with a garden, in a garden, satisfying our deep, deep longing to live this way—richness where it matters and simplicity where it matters."

In Australia, Eva was able to work full-time as an artist. Her paintings grew with her surroundings.

"At first I painted flowers, still-lifes with flowers, the gardens, and landscapes I experienced. And, on the rare weekends when Erwin was free of work, we would go camping in the countryside. The surroundings of Melbourne offered such variety: the city on its wide, lovely bay; out along the Mornington Peninsula, the huge oceanscape, surf, and stands of tea trees, eucalyptus, acacias, and lilly pilly trees. North of the city, and within an hour's drive, there's the moist rainforest with tree ferns, *Eucalyptus regnans*, growing up to a hundred metres, expanses of fragrant prostantheras at the forest edge. West of there, you find dry sclerophyll forests, and in between the moist and the dry there

Eva Diener, *Fata Morgana 1*, 2011, acrylic on canvas, 44 x 68 inches.

are areas of green pasture with huge, old eucalyptus trees here and there, like a savannah. Also, wide fields of grey, brown, red, or black soil, with windbreaks of eucalypts. We learned to identify all the different varieties. So exciting! Again, I revelled in the combination of botany, geology, and pure beauty. The more of this I experienced, the more I wanted to capture the bigger and more splendid landscapes in my work."

In 1973, after seven years in Australia, Erwin accepted an invitation to establish the Department of Immunology at the University of Alberta in Edmonton. For two people who had adored the mountains, lakes, and alpine vegetation of Switzerland, then were transported with delight by the monumental and exotic nature of Australia, Edmonton was, as Eva says, "difficult for us from a landscape point of view."

Despite the city's short growing season, they soon found deep fulfillment in this new phase of their lives.

The potential of rhododendrons in a woodland setting: A group of *R. roxieanum* and its variations, with *R. pachysanthum* in bloom.

"First, the campus was lovely. Erwin would walk through it to work, and I would hike and walk along the river valley and the campus, too. Our house, which had a good though neglected garden, was between the campus and the river valley. The potential was there, and in no time, this garden was alive again. It was like a beautiful island. There was even an old linden tree, just like those in so many cities of Europe. You lose your head in early summer with the lovely fragrance. Along the perimeter of the property, I claimed more and more of the ground and planted shrubs and perennials and annuals. It was very beautiful for the short three months that a garden gets in Edmonton."

When they'd been in Canada for a short while, the Dieners started visiting Vancouver.

"We loved the city. We walked around and around Stanley Park. We spent masses of time in the two botanical gardens and were fascinated by the lushness of their woodland areas. Here, for the first time, we encountered species rhododendrons. We'd *hated* rhododendrons before! Until then, we'd just seen them in bright reds and violets in showy gardens, and equated them with pink garden flamingos and ceramic dwarfs. The University of British Columbia's botanical garden not only had wonderful species rhododendrons, but they were growing in proper surroundings. We saw their potential and beauty in a woodland setting, just as we soon learned about all the other treasures that grow in the west coast habitat."

Further explorations of coastal British Columbia included a trip to the Sunshine Coast, a forty-minute ferry trip from West Vancouver.

"My brother was visiting from Switzerland and we wanted to show him the northwest Pacific coastal landscape. We searched for a place to stay where you could see and hear the water, but in the early 1970s, there was little public road access. From the pier in Roberts Creek, we noticed cottages along the water and thought, 'Maybe you have to buy a piece of land here in order to pitch your tent somewhere at the water's edge.'"

After much searching, they found the narrow wedge of land on which they now live.

"When we saw it, we gasped and said, 'This is what we want; this is *our* place, our rocky bluff!' One acre of glorious moss and rock, angled down to the water. At that point, our only desire was to have a piece of land on which to pitch our tiny tent for one or two weeks in the summers, and to be able to walk down the goat path to the sea and swim. And to return to Edmonton when the holiday was over—that's what we did for many years.

"We certainly didn't think of *ever* starting a garden—no, no, no! We were determined to spend our time here together, with each of us pursuing our respective work 100 percent. Not a square inch of garden to spoil this rock! That was the solemn promise we gave each other. It seems ridiculous now, considering what we've built and planted here over the years."

Over time, from their rocky campsite, the Dieners started to develop an affinity for the coastal forest. Realizing that there was very little mature, low-altitude forest left in the surrounding area, and that the forty-acre woodland beyond their plot had only been logged selectively, they knew it was worth saving. They approached the owner with an offer to purchase some of it. Eva

The discreet colours of Eva's woodland in spring. Left to right: *Rhododendron litiense*, *R. pachysanthum*, *R. sutchuenense*, with *Cercidiphyllum japonicum* (katsura) leafing out in foreground.

says, "I was reminded of the nature reserve my grandfather created in the early 1930s in Switzerland. I was determined to try and preserve this land with its still-healthy variety of mature trees."

In the course of their annual summer sojourns, Eva and Erwin formed the intention to retire eventually to the Sunshine Coast. Each year, they would restate their offer to the owner, who promised to hold part of the forest for their purchase. In the early 1980s, they built a simple house so that they could visit in the winter. Then, three years before their retirement, they received a call from a Sechelt neighbour, who told them the owner was clear-cutting the whole forest. They were devastated. On their next trip west, they viewed the wreckage and decided to add to their land by purchasing a portion of the clear-cut for planting just a few trees.

As they added to their original plot, they had to confront their determination *not* to become gardeners. Eva says, "In frustration and out of sadness for the loss of the forest, we decided to renounce our vow for one year only: sacrifice our work and assuage our sadness by starting a garden."

But the temptation to plant more and more grew and grew.

"I couldn't stop looking at beautiful books about English gardens and visiting nurseries and garden shops. We cleared out the glade below of all the broken-down, buried cars, car parts, washing machines, all overgrown with blackberries. We started by searching out mature rhododendrons for this

area—big-leaved species and no red or violet! With all the green, I wanted any colour to be discreet: white and off-white, soft yellow, light rose.

"For me, foliage comes first, whether in a woodland garden or a bouquet. Even when I buy a bouquet at the florist to bring to friends, I first start with the greenery before choosing perhaps three, four flowers. For me, it's about the greenery and just *some* colour. When we repeatedly wandered through the UBC garden, we rarely researched when the plants bloomed. We weren't looking for flowers; we were looking at form and particularly at the leaves—their shapes, shades, their richness and variety of greenness. So, here in our woodland, you see large-leafed, medium-leafed trees, and shrubs, each form chosen and allowed to develop consistent with its own nature and size."

Eva's vow to devote only one year to full-time garden building turned into three. She says she dreamt about resuming her painting but didn't, couldn't, do it. The garden had consumed her creatively and aesthetically.

"The garden had become the focus of my creative urge. By that time, we had already added to the rocky bluff where our house stands. We had learned to our horror that the nearby perfect stand of coastal forest was also slated for clear-cutting and must be saved. Two more acres, we thought, would make a botanical garden."

As gardener and as artist, Eva Diener channels nature, using artifice where required, to create what she calls an amalgam.

Top: *Weigela florida* 'Foliis Purpureis' (left) *Calycanthus florida* (right).

Above: The natural landscape that inspired the dry meadow.

Opposite: The dry garden in late spring.

"To offset the woodland and complete the main part of the garden, we needed an open plain, a meadow, but *definitely* not a lawn, and not a landscape needing watering. One boundary of the area we had in mind already had a long, beautiful rock, formed into wavelike shapes by receding glaciers of the last ice age. I thought, 'Lovely! I want longish, mounded beds to echo the rock, with the same flowing shapes.' So I walked, trailing a ribbon behind me, to trace the narrow paths which would also define the contours I wanted in the beds. Xeriscape gardening hadn't been popularized yet, but it was this idea, of course. So I decided to plant rosemary, thyme, salvias, lavenders, certain small dianthus, oregano, and three species of scabious. Without special preparation, these plants would have difficulty surviving our wet winters, so I had to buy truckloads of sand to create the mounds. This meant I had to haul a few hundred wheelbarrows of sand!"

Now, framed by a group of tall trees, these dry beds mimic the movement of the rock undulating at the side. They invite the eye.

Eva is enthralled. "The naturalized thyme and the salvias, the dianthus, the daisies, the scabious, and a host of other flowers, dying in some areas, thriving in others, as in the wild, alongside the moss and lichens growing on the rocks—such harmony."

In addition, the great variety of flowering plants helps the propagation of different species of butterflies, native bees, bumblebees, and other insects. (Elsewhere in the garden, the small pond harbours a population of amphibians, including red-legged frogs, tree frogs, long-toed salamanders, and a species of newt.)

Helleborus foetidus.

"And now, in spring, you see the Corsican hellebore [*Helleborus argutifolius*] and the tiny yellow *Tulipa sylvestris*—exquisite in this situation. They say, 'Plant the tulips in a big mass.' Actually, I like them better sparingly in a landscape, as in the wild. I'm also very, very fond of the variety of greens found here in the flowers and foliage of *Helleborus foetidus* and *argutifolius*.

"As I see it, in the garden, small landscapes have to be as complete as possible so as to create the beautiful big landscape. Since childhood, I have learned to appreciate the variety, distinctiveness and differences of nature, changing with the seasons.

"I carry the landscape within me."

Eva Diener, *Garden*, 2011, acrylic on canvas, 68 x 50 inches. After several years of total concentration on the garden, Eva resumed painting during the winter months. A collection of some of her new paintings was exhibited at the Galerie ArtSeefeld in Zürich in 2011.

The misty colours of the 'Chosin Gallery garden in winter.

FOUR

Nature by Design

"I AM A POTTER *AND* a gardener. I am a gardener *and* a potter."

Robin Hopper clasps his hands tightly, emphasizing that, for him, the two are inseparable faces of the same coin.

"I started working with clay at the age of three, while Hitler was bombing the hell out of London. London is built on clay, so as the bombs fell, down came the houses and up came the clay, and I would play with it all day and make little objects. Rocks were revealed too, and, looking back, I see that as a child I was beginning to work with, and to understand, the mineral materials that both the potter and the gardener work with. So to me, pottery and gardening are totally enmeshed. *Totally.* They're using the same minerals. The geological aspect of clay and the geological aspect of being a gardener are one and the same. Moreover, they're using the same concept of space."

Robin and his wife, Judi Dyelle, also a potter, live and work in Metchosin, near Victoria, BC. They have separate studios. As he works, he listens to jazz and classics; she likes middle-of-the-road music.

Metchosin, Robin explains, means "place of stinking fish," the name given by the original inhabitants in commemoration of a beached whale that, long ago, rotted malodorously on the shore. Robin and Judi call their home 'Chosin Pottery, an abbreviation that sounds Japanese, which is fitting because, as we soon found out, Robin's gardening—as well as his potting—is greatly influenced by the Japanese tradition.

"It's interesting," notes Robin, "that in Japan the two most valued art forms are gardening and pottery. In North America, the *least* appreciated art forms are gardening and pottery. Gardening is an art, *absolutely*. In fact, I feel that the development of this garden is the most gratifying artwork I have ever done or expect to do."

Art and nature in Robin Hopper's garden: old-growth firs and a glimpse of borrowed landscape; the fan, a symbol of authority in Japan; masks peering from the rugged bark.

Robin was living in Ontario in the mid-1970s when he bought the place, sight unseen. From photographs and a realtor's description, he knew it was exactly what he wanted.

"This is one of the last privately owned pieces of property on southern Vancouver Island that has first-growth Douglas fir. There's an organization, the Heritage Tree Foundation, and they've registered this site. That bigleaf maple over there is a heritage tree too—one of the largest on the coast. And there are tons of native plants here, including a significant number of Garry oaks. We have a fraction under six acres, of which the garden now takes up almost half, bordered on all sides by native forest and wildflower meadow. I've always been a gardener and this property was the perfect place for what I wanted to do. There was a semi-derelict house, built in 1905, which was restored, and I started the garden about thirty-five years ago.

"When I first came, much of the land was an automobile graveyard. Dead trucks, dead cars, dead everything. And once I'd got all that hauled away, I started in on the blackberries. It took me a year to clean it out, and once that was done it was amazing, the wildflowers that popped up: shooting stars, chocolate lilies, pink and white fawn lilies. Then I met some of the rhododendron growers in Victoria, people who were growing plants from seed collected in China, and they said to me, 'You've got a great place here for growing rhododendrons. Do you need any?' And I was thinking maybe they were talking of cuttings. 'Oh no,' they said, 'big ones, ten feet high. You dig. You take.' Well, it turned out they were growing in urban gardens and had to be moved for lack of space. Some of these species grow huge, to forty feet or more, even up to a hundred in the foothills of the Himalayas. So I rented a couple of pickup trucks and rounded up a few guys and we dug up and brought in a hundred and fifty rhododendron shrubs. And now they're up to twenty feet high, so it's pretty spectacular through here in spring."

Rhododendron 'Sir Charles Lemon'.

Robin has coined the term "Anglo–Japanadian" to characterize his garden. Anglo reflects his own heritage, and his sense of humour, manifested in touches of wit and whimsy here and there in the garden. Japan refers to the overall influence of that culture, while Canadian represents the setting and the integration of native plants.

"This is *not* a Japanese garden, but it owes a lot to that tradition. I've researched and studied Japanese gardens, largely because of the interaction with Japanese ceramics, especially the way they use ceramics in the garden. There are five styles.

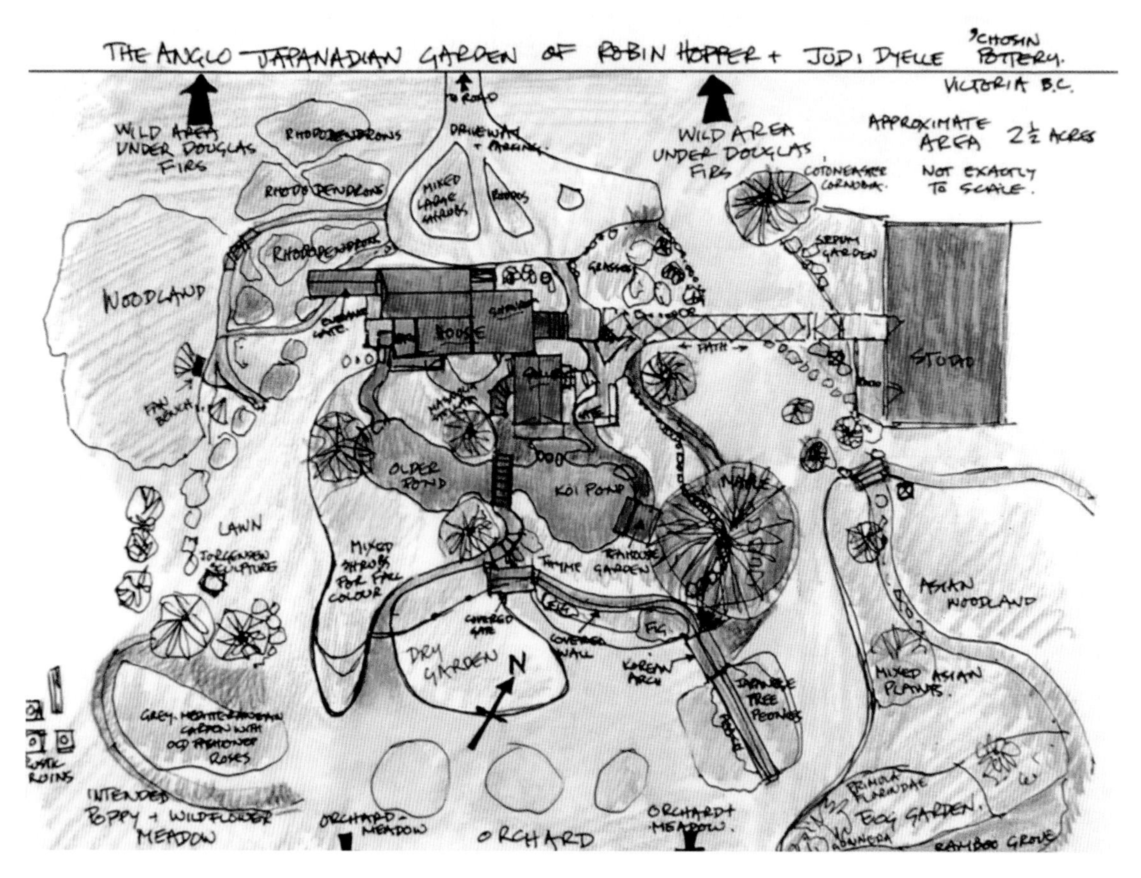

The garden map, drawn by Robin Hopper.

"The largest, made for the Samurai nobility, is the stroll garden. It has long, meandering pathways and large features such as a lake, with different landscapes opening up as you walk.

"Second, there's the scroll garden. These are inspired by Chinese paintings that are made on scrolls. As you unwind the scroll a little more is revealed, like going round the corner in a garden and finding something new.

"Third, there's the courtyard garden, the *tsuboniwa*, a small enclosure within high walls but open to the sky. It may include a small pool or a patio, some carefully selected rocks, as well as plants and ceramics.

"Fourth, there's the *roji*, or tea garden, which traditionally surrounds Japanese tea houses and is of course associated with the tea ceremony. First, guests enter the *machiya*, a waiting room, then they pass through a small

Above left: A glimpse of light through the rhododendron forest.

Above right: Randomly self-seeded fawn lilies and hellebores, running wild.

opening, which requires bending low and symbolically separates the quiet of the tea room from the noisy world without.

"Finally there's the Zen garden, which is a highly symbolic, abstract, contemplative space usually made very simply of rock, sand, and gravel.

"This garden owes a lot to all five styles. I want something that's relatively natural, so that if the weeds are there or something dies, and you don't get a chance to prune stuff back when it's dead, it doesn't matter that much because that's the way it is in nature. When I come to a place like this, with the old-growth trees and so on, I don't want to spoil it. I want to make use of what belongs naturally: the native plants and trees and the layout they suggest. I want to enhance it, but not impose some formal layout, which you so often find in large European gardens. I try to make it feel as though it was always here."

We entered the garden through a gate off the circular driveway and plunged into a mature rhododendron forest, the overhead foliage mingling with other trees and native shrubs, set off against the craggy bark of old-growth Douglas firs. The forest floor is all happy chaos: hostas mingling with hellebores (*H. foetidus*) in flower, the leaves of hardy cyclamen, bits of iris, various self-seeded woodland wildlings, and, most delightfully, the flowers of the white fawn lily (*Erythronium oregonum*). Birds and bugs must love this place. All appears wholly natural, and indeed, here, nature now takes its course, though along lines originally conceived and designed not by nature but by the gardener, Robin.

A concrete pathway (which Robin says symbolizes a river) meanders through this woodland. Halfway along, the concrete is cast in fan shapes. Robin explains, "In Asian gardens, the fan is a symbol of authority, as well as

Art and Robin's sense of fun enchant the visitor to the 'Chosin Gallery garden.

knowledge and learning, and I teach and write books, so I figure I'm entitled to do this."

At this point, a trio of life-sized ceramic torsos stands, as if in conversation, in a pretty patch of yellow epimedium.

"These were made by a Danish artist at a workshop in Banff who realized she couldn't possibly afford to ship them home. I paid her for the cost of materials and brought them here. They're actually quite lightweight, so I half-filled them with sand so they won't blow over.

"So this is an obvious example of a scroll garden; turn the corner and another picture unfolds."

And the picture that now unfolds is full of humour.

"The kids love it when they come around the corner and see these mega-toadstools.

"We have busloads of people coming from different garden clubs and so on, and when they come along here they see this and ask, 'What is this flower?' and I say, 'It's *Florus ceramicus hybridus robiniae* and they get their notebooks out and write it down. And a few minutes later they realize I'm having them on. But you know, bamboo can be pretty boring stuff and you need some sort of flower to set it off. And this of course blooms all year round!"

Left and next page: Robin, the potter, makes jokes in clay for his garden.

Florus ceramicus hybridus robiniae.

The "dogwood tree."

"A few years ago we had a really, really bad windstorm through here. There were gusts up to a hundred miles an hour. This was a red cherry, and the wind just tore it apart. I didn't want to take it out altogether, so I cut it way back. Now, I call it the dogwood tree."

One of the pleasing aspects of Robin's garden is the way in which he incorporates ceramics, ironwork, wood, and stone. He works them into the landscape, integrated as if they were plants rather than ornaments or *objets d'art* demanding individual attention. Like the plants, they *belong*, as if they had grown there, emerging out of the ground or out of the bark as naturally as the flowers and foliage they accompany. As with the plants, in Robin's hands these pieces are no more than elements of a larger creative work, his garden. Thus, as the artist intends, the whole is a work of art, as distinct from a garden featuring works of art.

WE EMERGED FROM the woodland shade as the "river" path poured us onto a small lawn, the "ocean."

"You have choices now," says Robin. "You can go back upriver, or south through that hole in the wall, the moon gate. You can go that way toward the

The emperor's gate.

house, which symbolizes civilization, or that way, through the entrance gate. All big Japanese gardens have an entrance gate reserved for the emperor. The best we've had is the Queen's representative in Victoria!"

We chose the sunlit moon gate, for the promise it held of new surprises, and encountered a truly original feature: the entrance of a long, dark tunnel, its frame a row of iron hoops interwoven with strips of thin wooden lath.

"I wanted to create a transition between the woodland shade and the part of the garden that's in sun all day long. So I came up with what I call the gladiatorial tunnel, as in ancient Rome. When the gladiators entered the arena, they did so through a blind-ended tunnel, with twists and turns which began in some dark assembly room and ended in the blinding sun of the arena. It's the same here. You can't see what's at the end of it until you get there, though you can get a hint by peeking through the slats. Children just love it.

"Then you come out here into a high-perfume area. There are rugosa roses and five different honeysuckle vines that cover this rotunda. The pillars are driftwood. The roof is an obsolete, ten-foot satellite dish, which the TV company gave me for free—and free is my favourite price. And being parabolic, it has the most amazing acoustics. If you stand in the middle and sing, you instantly transform yourself into an opera star. The floor is made with little bits of different-coloured leftover clay which I pressed flat and fired. Some of them have fossils in them."

Robin Hopper, potter and gardener, at the entrance of his "gladiatorial tunnel."

THE HEART OF the 'Chosin Gallery garden includes elements of both the *tsuboniwa*, or walled courtyard garden, and the *roji*, or tea garden. It is framed by the house and by a high, Japanese-style stucco wall, topped with a narrow cedar roof and a tangle of flowering vines. Within this space are two large lily ponds, separated by a wooden bridge. Two bronze cranes are courting by the bridge, perhaps eyeing the koi that lazily bottom-feed in the water below. Very lazily, it turns out. These koi are ceramic. In the summer, says Robin, both pools are full of water lilies, "a do-it-yourself Monet."

A *machiya*, or waiting room, beautifully situated, overlooks the lily pond. It is a sanctuary of pure serenity and, in the thin April sun, we sat with Robin to hear more about his sources of inspiration and how gardening relates to other spatial arts.

The rotunda, with its parabolic roof smothered in honeysuckle.
PHOTO JUDI DYELLE

The *machiya*, a place for quiet conversation.

"My parents were not gardeners. I didn't pick it up from them. But I've always been interested. I lived in South London, not far from a large park, and right close to that was a nursery, the venerable Veitch Nursery, which goes back to the nineteenth century. Many of the great hybrid rhododendrons had been created there from species grown from seed collected by plant hunters who worked for the founder, James Veitch. When I was about seventeen, I used to spend a lot of time drawing and sketching in that nursery and the adjacent park gardens, and through that began to become sharply aware of space and the use of space, or contrived space, in relation to garden themes.

In summer, these bottom-feeding ceramic koi will be hidden by water lilies—"a do-it-yourself Monet."

"As an artist, I'm concerned with physical space, or manipulated space, or visualized physical space. That's the artist's mind working—fitting physical things into specific spaces, particularly architecture—and I was very interested in both architecture and plants. As a child I wanted to do so many things, and becoming a landscape gardener was high on the list, but I never got around to that one and became a potter instead—which is manipulating space as a sculptor would, but in miniature, of course.

"I was also in theatre for quite some time. I was trained in theatre design, and as far as I'm concerned, a garden is a bloody great big theatre! Just as you create illusions in the theatre, so you create illusions in a garden. I mean, think

"A garden is a bloody big theatre."

of it as set design. You've got all these low-level things in the foreground and the big backdrop scenery; then you get the hanging vines, like the drapery which hangs over the stage—it's like one big theatre!

"My concept of a garden is quite different from most people's. For me, a garden is a physical space that has meaning. It is *not* a museum of flowers. The average garden tends to be a museum of flowers set out in a line, much the same as pots are lined up in museums all over the world. You know, 'Here's one of this and here's one of that . . .' and so on. When people lay out bedding plants or shrubs in a line, to my mind they're regimenting something which is naturally not regimented. I try to work with nature. Even so, there's a lot of structure in this garden, and it's not entirely dependent on flowers and foliage. Gardens that are entirely plant matter don't always look that interesting. A garden is a work of nature and a work of design, I believe."

Nature and design work together throughout Robin's garden. They work together at the steps leading up to the gallery.

"I like the movement of the stairs that first takes your eye and then your body up to the gallery."

They work together at the sheltered wooden bench in the middle of the Asian woodland—a sublime creation of nature and design.

"There's a particularly beautiful tea garden in Kyoto, where they have a gateway right in the middle of the garden. There's no pathway to it, there's no pathway from it. It's just *there*. This is *Zen* thinking. And I just loved its shape; it looked like an upturned boat. Well, I didn't want another gate, but I needed somewhere to sit and enjoy this part of the garden, so I built a boat-shaped roof over the bench here, and now it's naturalizing beautifully with the old cedar shingles, spattered with moss."

A sprawling fig tree frames the Korean arch.

Again, nature and design work together at the Korean arch that leads the visitor into the Asian woodland. An old fig tree sprawls beside this arch.

"We get hundreds of figs off this every year. It's on a south-facing wall that retains a lot of warmth. That tree will probably be the death of me, because I'm diabetic and figs have the highest sugar content of any fruit, they say. But what a way to go! I don't care! In summer, I can't walk past without picking one."

Indeed, Robin believes that a garden should appeal to every sense.

"The eye, obviously; the ear catches the sound of trickling water and of course birdsong and the breeze in the trees. Scent is very important for me; even in winter there's witch hazel. Then, when spring brings on the blossom and the fragrance, I try to place plants, such as viburnums, so that you're *assailed* by scent as you stroll through the garden. Even touch: the felty feel of the indumentum on the underside of a rhododendron leaf; the craggy bark of an old-growth fir; the cool, satiny skin of the ceramic torsos, back in the forest."

Robin explains that in the Japanese tradition, a garden, if you know how to "read" it, may tell the story of the person who owns it: the battles he has fought, his travels and experiences. So many of the features in his garden recall his own travels in Asia. The moon gate is a familiar feature of Chinese architecture. The archway that tapers from the top to the bottom is typical of Korean architecture. The pattern of paving stones is borrowed from one of the best-known Japanese gardens, Tofuku-ji in Kyoto, where Robin admired the perfection of the checkerboard of granite and deep moss. These and other elements reflect his experiences and memories over a life of seven decades and counting.

Robin's "tongue-in-cheek" Zen garden.

We walked through the Asian woodland—a rambunctious forest of bamboo, witch hazel, azaleas, ornamental cherries, magnolias, and Japanese maples, with an understorey of ferns, hellebores, grasses, and many competing ground covers—and finally came to a work that brilliantly illustrates Robin's flair as a potter, as well as his somewhat irreverent sense of fun.

"In Japan, Zen gardens often have a dry stream and waterfalls, simply sand and gravel. Of course, the trouble with sand and gravel here is that needles and leaves and spent flowers are constantly raining from the trees and shrubs above, so it's impossible to keep it neat and tidy as it should be. So I have

The ’Chosin Gallery garden in fall.
PHOTO JUDI DYELLE

what I call my 'tongue-in-cheek' Zen garden. It has a hundred brightly coloured, ceramic koi in a cement stream. Ninety-two of them are swimming downstream and the other eight represent me, swimming upstream, against the current. Swirling patterns of stones suggest the flow of the stream. The whole thing can be simply hosed down or swept clean."

Again, even in this work of clay and concrete, nature and design are beginning to work together, as moss starts to take on the role of pond weed. Eventually, nature will have its way. Perhaps, decades from now, some future owner of this heritage land will scrape away layers of salal, blackberries, weeds, and leaf mould to rediscover Robin's "tongue-in cheek" Zen garden. The concrete may crumble away, but the koi will endure for a thousand years.

"As for the future of this garden, well, I don't worry about that. Unlike my work as a potter, what I have created as a gardener is ephemeral. It cannot have permanence. It tells the story of my life and my travels and my beliefs. Beyond that, it can only exist in memory or, for a while, in pictures or words in books like yours. When they take me off in a paddy wagon, I shall not look back. I have never looked back. Others will take up this property and do what they want with it.

"Meantime, all I can say is a lot of people enjoy coming here—and seem to enjoy it more than highly structured, perfectly maintained, public show gardens."

Helleborus argutifolius 'Pacific Frost'.

FIVE

Pacific Frost

PACIFIC FROST IS A HELLEBORE, a variation of the Corsican hellebore (*H. argutifolius* 'Pacific Frost'). At the height of its popularity, around 2005, it was mass-produced and mass-marketed with paeans of praise: "truly unique," "the darling of many a collector." Since then, like most passing fancies, it has moved to the back of the shelf, though it's still available and sought after by hellebore enthusiasts. In its heyday, it made solid profits for nurseries in North America and Europe—though not for its originator, the redoubtable Vancouver gardener Pam Frost.

"Well, when they were redoing the perennial garden at the University of British Columbia's president's house, they gave all those plants—which mostly came from Blooms of Bressingham in England—to the man in charge of the grounds, Ken Wilson. He was retiring and wanted to propagate them for a little nursery he was setting up. So I was looking at plants there and saw he had a line of Corsican hellebore seedlings, and I said, 'Oh, look, there's one that's variegated.' (At that time I was very keen on variegation—if it was variegated, I'd buy it. Rather gone off it now.) He said, 'Yes, but I think it's a virus. I'm going to throw it out.' So I said, 'Please, may I buy it?' And he sold it to me for two dollars. Then I kept it isolated out front where there weren't any other hellebores and one year it set seed, and the babies were practically all variegated like the parent. So I thought it couldn't be a virus. The variegation was in the genes.

"Then word got around that I had this plant and I was getting phone calls from people as far away as Wisconsin. So I wrote to the British hellebore specialist Will McLewin, and he said, 'This is a new variety—you should introduce it properly.' So that's what happened; it was formally registered with the help of the Hardy Plant Society. It was Stephen Lacey, a British garden writer, who came up with the name, 'Pacific Frost'."

'Pacific Frost' is a freak, like many new plants the result of a chance mutation in a garden or, in this case, a nursery. It's an outstanding example of variegation in plants, with dark-green leaves heavily speckled (frosted) in white, and clusters of ivory blooms in late winter. Has Pam Frost "gone off" this plant?

She replies with a chuckle and characteristic emphasis, "Well, I like it because it's a bit personal to me, *but actually not that much*. Partly because now I only like variegation where it's clean and clearly defined—stripes, for instance. I don't like mottling very much and that's really what it is. But I am attached to it. It's never grown as vigorously as the parent. But if it's in the shade, it's perfectly healthy. I've heard people say it doesn't do very well, but my original plant only died last year. I had it for twenty years."

Pam lives and gardens on a quiet, leafy street in a part of Vancouver that would have been the western outskirts when the house was built in 1911.

"The previous owners asked the architect, Ron Thom, to draw up a design for them in 1953 to add a small second floor, with a bedroom, study, and bathroom, and sort of give it a fifties look. There had been a veranda all across the front and one at the back, which he incorporated into the house. We bought it in 1968 and added another bedroom and study in the front upstairs. We've lived here ever since."

And in that time, Pam's garden and her creative gardening skills—along with her legendary knowledge of plants—have together grown into one of the most admired private settings in the Pacific Northwest. All the more surprising, then, that unlike many great gardeners, she was not born with a trowel in her hand.

"My mother gardened. She was a very keen gardener. But I wasn't interested, *not at all*. My mother tried to encourage me. I remember her taking me around and telling me all the plant names, and she set aside little patches for my brother and me to make our own gardens, but I wasn't *really* interested. I remember I was fond of primroses—still am—and I planted some of those, but that's about it. Come to think of it, my mother probably found my lack of interest disappointing. No, I wasn't really interested until after I came to

Canada in 1956, after David and I were married and had our own place in Vancouver."

David Frost, also an immigrant from England, was a professor of chemistry at the University of British Columbia, where Pam worked.

"It was a rented house and we didn't want to interfere with someone else's garden, so all I grew was vegetables and a few herbs. It wasn't until we bought *this* house that I *really* became interested. So of course what we have here has evolved over forty-five years. As you see, the lots along this street are exceptionally deep. There was no garden here behind the house, just a very long strip of grass the width of the lot and about two hundred and fifty feet long. And it looked awful. *Awful.* Just *grass* and a few trees. Nothing else. We had a blank canvas. By then we had two small children and a dog, so we put fences along the side. And it *still looked awful.*

"I started to plant some shrubs along the edges to hide the fence, but really, we didn't have that much money for the garden. However, we were going home to England to see family and friends every couple of years and I went to Chelsea and other flower shows and they'd have these lists of *wonderful plants*, none of which I knew and anyway you couldn't get them in Vancouver. So that's when I started growing things from *seed.* I joined the Royal Horticultural Society and sent for seed, which they collected in their gardens in Britain and provided free to members. That was fun and I tried anything that sounded appealing, though of course it took a few years to get a shrub or tree to flowering size. *Very* satisfying though, when you've grown it yourself from seed. I still have four large rhododendron species, which I started from RHS seed in the early 1970s.

"Of course, everything was listed in botanical Latin and I had to learn that. But Latin was my favourite subject at school. I used to read Latin, and this helped enormously when somebody rattled off the name of a plant, because you're getting a description of colour or size or leaf shape or something. I can understand that some people think it's *rather pedantic* to use the proper names, but it can be so confusing if you don't know the scientific name because it's a *very precise* way of identifying a plant. You know *exactly* what you're getting and you can read a label in any part of the world and know what you're looking at, even if you don't know a word of the local language. I remember once

Pam's garden in May—beauty and serenity as far as the eye can see. The anchoring robinia, on the right, has not yet leafed out.

David brought a visiting scholar from China home to dinner. He couldn't speak English and I couldn't speak Chinese, so we talked about trees in botanical Latin and got on just fine!"

FROM PAM'S STREET, there's nothing to indicate the remarkable garden that stretches from the back of the house to the seemingly distant limits of the property. We climbed the steps and were welcomed at the front door, then led through the house (noting, along the way, the botanical prints decorating the walls) to the back door, which opens onto a deck and the thrill of the first overview of Pam's garden.

There's an immediate sense of detachment from the world outside, of stepping into a green retreat of rest and serenity. In our imagination, we saw the perfect setting for an elegant English garden party—couples strolling arm in arm, ladies with parasols, champagne. Pam's landscape is self-contained,

What a difference a month makes! Pam's garden in June, with the *Robinia pseudoacacia* balanced on the left by a dogwood (*Cornus kousa*) in bloom.

without any dependence on borrowed views beyond. Neighbouring houses do not intrude. The eye follows the curving lawn—cunningly mown by David in swaths that repeat the arc of the borders. The lawn seems to vanish, then reappear farther on. There's an illusion that it goes on forever, lost in the backdrop of large conifers standing on the property beyond. A *trompe l'oeil.* Trees and shrubs work together in harmony, a chorus led by a striking *Robinia pseudoacacia*, planted in exactly the right place, halfway along.

"That Robinia, the big one, I saw it in Chelsea in 1974 and thought, 'I *want* one of those,' but you couldn't get it here, of course, so I asked if they could ship it and they said they could. So I got one, just a sapling, and there it is now, a beautiful tree with leaves the colour of chartreuse that immediately draw the eye. And as it grew, I thought, 'What I need is another one to balance it, farther down on the other side.' But by then you could get them here."

No landscape consultant had a hand in the development of Pam's garden. She began with no fixed idea of where it all might lead. She describes, rather, a process of evolving discovery and inspiration, influenced by the plants she found and the gardeners she met and admired.

"By that time I'd joined the Alpine Garden Club of BC and got to know some of the *really good* gardeners here, such as Margaret Charlton and Francisca Darts. Francisca's garden was like a treasure trove. She had these wonderful plants and trees, and I'd make a note of the names and look for the plants or try to grow them from seed. Beth Chatto is another source of inspiration I must mention. The way she uses plants in her Essex garden has influenced me a great deal. I also loved exchanging plants and ideas with Susan Ryley in Victoria. She was a wonderful, creative gardener and a very good friend.

A painterly composition, anchored by *Hosta sieboldiana*.

"At one point I did draw a map to scale and that's when I saw how very long and thin it looked, and I realized I didn't want a long tunnel, but nor did I want to break it up into compartments. That *didn't* appeal to me because it's so *restful* looking all the way down to the end. But I didn't know quite how to do it. There were three apple trees in a line halfway down and the first thing I did was take out the middle one—it was right in the centre. Then I took out a half-dead dogwood and a diseased cherry tree. I thought, 'If I'm going to make it easy for David to mow, I can't leave these trees isolated in the grass,' so that helped decide what needed to be taken out. I wanted the trees that were left to become *part of the garden*. So that influenced the winding shape of the lawn. I used to lay out a hose and cut along the curve it made to widen the beds. Over time it has changed a lot, but very gradually, a foot at a time, no more than that. There was never a grand design. This garden has evolved over forty-five years. I still occasionally cut little bits out of the grass to give more room for plants. Just a spadeful. Cut it out, turn it over, add a bit of compost. That's it.

"Then I got involved in the annual plant sale at the VanDusen Botanical Garden. I knew a bit about trees and shrubs but nothing about perennials, so I volunteered for that and learned on the job and soon found myself in charge of the perennial section. And of course there was the Alpine Garden Club. And doing it. Experimenting. Trying new seeds. Cuttings too. A lot of trial and error.

A canvas including *Hosta* 'Francee', *Adiantum pedatum* (a fern), and *Hakonechloa macra* (a grass).

Of course, not everything worked. That's the nature of experiment. But things I was able to grow successfully from seeds or cuttings, if I *liked* them, became part of this garden.

"I've had *crazes* for plants. I'd get to like a particular genus, and I'd want to grow every species and variety. Done that with geraniums, euphorbias, hostas, corydalis, arisaemas, hellebores. I don't do that anymore, but I have something of all of them. I find it *very* difficult to get rid of plants, but I had to let some of them go!"

David Tarrant, garden writer and broadcaster, has been a regular visitor to Pam's garden. "In many ways the garden reflects Pam's calm nature," he says. "As I see her ever-evolving creation, I become quite excited and animated, while Pam smiles, remains calm, and points out some of her particular favourite plants. And every time, I'm immediately struck by the serenity of her gorgeous garden—a long, narrow city lot alive with a soft symphony of colours, flowing away in perfectly managed curving borders. Much of the colour is often from flowers, but it's the extraordinary variety of foliage shapes and sizes which completes the soothing tapestry. It's totally pleasing to the eye.

An inspired collation of colour and shape.

"I think Pam's ever-watchful artistic inner eye—seeking out plants which either flower at the same time, or have stunning complementary foliage at the same time—can picture them growing together. She *paints* with her plants."

Exactly so. David Tarrant gets to the essence of her artistry with plants. It's no surprise to learn that Pam is indeed a painter. She paints landscapes in oil. "I'd love to do botanical painting, but I can't do watercolours."

There was a long pause as she thought about the source of her ideas.

"I really don't know how I decide if a thing looks right or not. I suppose painting certainly helps one look at things. The real fun side is putting plants together—you know, balance, texture, colour—especially the leaves, because the flowers don't last that long. It's the way things *look* together. But I really can't tell you how it works. Trouble is, I don't analyze these things. I just know when it's right. I love ferns, for example. Put them with a nice simple leaf, a hosta, say. I look at the garden and think, 'Oh I just need a bit of *that* over *there*.' It's *instinctive*. I have a dicentra [bleeding heart] down there in a pot.

The leaves have a bit of blue, an unusual olive colour. And I've walked around with it and placed it here and there, in cool, semi-shade areas where it should do well, and looked at it and it never seems *quite right*. So it's still in the pot because I can't in my mind find just the right place for it.

"I don't very often go out and choose a plant for a particular place. I'll usually buy something because I love it, and then I'll walk it around the garden and find the right place. On the other hand, if a plant is expensive, or difficult to get, or I really care about it, I'll put it for the first year in a place I know it's going to grow and be happy as much as possible. And then I might move it. I think it's useful to know where plants come from to know where they'll do best in the garden."

Are there colours Pam doesn't want in the garden or doesn't like?

She considers this carefully. "I'm not terribly keen on that *very sad pink*. Can't describe it. Or mustard yellow."

Mustard yellow: a fine sight in a field of canola or a late-spring meadow of buttercups and dandelions. But in a garden it can be discordant, shrieking, "Look at me, look over here." It's an outlaw colour. It does not blend and definitely would not look right in Pam's subtle weaving of flower and foliage. Some gardeners eschew yellow entirely, but not Pam. She loves the soft yellow of the large single blooms of *Paeonia mlokosewitschii*, with the hint of red rimming the young leaves. As for that *very sad pink*, just exactly what her eye sees is left to our imagination. Perhaps it's the stain of blue in the colour as pink merges into mortuary mauve?

"I know I have too many plants in the garden. I *know* that. It could be a bit busy. Which is why the grass is very helpful because it's plain. It helps to tie everything together. So at one time I thought, 'I'll discipline myself and I'll have all the same colours together,' because you've still got the variety of shapes and forms but not colour, so it wouldn't be such a jumble, but I'm afraid I've rather given up on that."

A walk with Pam around her garden is not unlike walking through an art gallery, the plant paintings framed in the camera. Rather than drawing attention to individual plants, she evaluates the mix, the collage of contrasting and complementary shapes and colours of plant combinations.

Pam Frost is renowned for her artistry in blending form and colour of flower and foliage in her garden.

"My garden is not *perfect*. It's a work in progress. But I really like the way some of the shapes are working together. I make notes all the time. I go round the whole garden at least once a week and make notes about what looks quite good and what *doesn't* and what I have to move.

"There's something going on all through the year. And I quite like the textures I've put in. I *like* it. It's not necessarily what anybody else likes. But I just enjoy these different leaves. I think it works.

"I like picking up the colours from leaves in the flowers. But it's always

changing because some things do well so they *get too big*, and you've got to change them. I'm always moving the furniture, changing them around. Poor things! And one thing I really like about plants is who they remind you of when you go around the garden.

"Don Armstrong gave me a lot of plants, and they're really special. He was a great plantsman. He didn't live too far from here. Don gave me that giant lily [*Cardiocrinum giganteum* var *yunnanense*]. It dies after flowering but has quite a few offsets, so it keeps on flowering most years."

Pam laughingly and affectionately remembers another great gardener, Vera Peck. "She was a force to be reckoned with! She *loved* alpines, so she'd come here and declare, 'All you grow is *cabbages*! You should have a *scree*.' She was always giving me plants. I was very fond of her—but *she wouldn't like this at all*!"

Pam herself is no less a force to be reckoned with. Her friend Beverley Merryfield (herself an admired, creative gardener) recalls their first encounter. "Back in the mid-1990s, I can remember going on study weekends, put on by the Vancouver Hardy Plant Group, and meeting Pam. Somebody had said to me, 'Glue on to someone who knows a lot—like Pam Frost—and keep your mouth shut and your ears open. And you will learn.' And I have. She's greatly enriched my appreciation of plants and how to use them. I'd never seen her garden when I first met her, only heard about it, and I was dying to see it. So I was thrilled when I got an invitation, and oh, I was astounded! There were so many plants I didn't know. I felt like Alice in Wonderland.

"I admire the strength of her conviction about plants. She has a very clear idea of what she wants. One day when she was fussing and fuming about where to place things—and she'd gone on a little while—I said, 'Would you ever consider getting somebody else's opinion?' Well, she just about took my head off! Then—I'll never forget—we were taking Helen Dillon around Pam's garden and she showed us a variegated honeysuckle, the evergreen one, 'Baggesen's Gold'. I *hate* it. And Pam asked me what I thought of it and of course I didn't have the nerve to say.

"Yes, she can be a bit intimidating. Very strong personality. Straight to the point. She's got such a memory—she knows the names of everything—and she's quick to correct you if you get it wrong. But—great warmth and generosity. She's been very supportive of the hardy plant group. When I was running it, any time I wanted advice or an opinion she was the first one I'd turn to. She's been a major supporter of VanDusen Gardens for years. She used to be a guide there and was very involved in their big spring plant sale. She still works on plant labelling for them every Tuesday afternoon. And of course her support of the Alpine Garden Club of BC is legendary. She organized the seed exchange for years. A *huge* job!

In spring, a sublime tapestry of Lenten roses (*Helleborus x hybridus*).

"Pam is a superb plantswoman. I think all those, whether professional or amateur, who really care about gardening at its very best would agree with that. I just wish I had known her longer. She's had a big influence on me. In fact, Pam has had a big influence on many of us. I can't imagine any thoughtful gardener walking around Pam's garden with eyes open *not* reflecting on their own efforts—trying to see their work through *her* eyes, and wondering, 'What would Pam think of this?'"

Despite the very carefully considered placing of her plants, Pam loves to take advantage of happy accidents.

"Yes, I have a lot of self-sowing. For instance, this sea holly, 'Miss Willmott's Ghost'. They go on year after year. And I pull them out if they're not right. And the other thing that's a really good self-sower is this purple orach. It's also known as 'mountain spinach' and a red leaf or two adds a nice touch to a salad.

Clematis viticella 'Betty Corning'.

It grows up to about five feet, but of course it *never* comes up where I want it, so I have to move them to the right place. And I collect the seeds of the annual opium poppies and scatter them where I want them. But they don't necessarily co-operate. Like one year, I had a lovely poppy with single flowers in a lovely shade of grape—it's called 'Lauren's Grape'. It came up with this blue hosta. *Just perfect.* But never again, even though every year I scatter the seed in the same place.

"There's serendipity too in the way that clematis grow. All mine clamber up other plants. I have a lot of viticellas, because those clematis are really easy and wonderful scramblers. Like 'Betty Corning'—do you know her? She's bluish and rambles up that yellow privet. It's a nice combination."

Despite its use as a folk remedy for curing croup in chickens and its other, better authenticated medicinal properties, few gardeners would bother growing rue. For one thing, the flowers are inconspicuous. But Pam is not like most other gardeners. She looks at plants in a different way and values blue rue's feathery leaves and their potential for blending and weaving with other foliage.

"Yes, I'm much happier working with foliage. I had a blue rue, which I brought thirty-five years ago from my mother's garden in Sussex. I grew it in company with *Hypericum* 'Elstead' variety and *Senecio greyii*, which had the bad taste to have yellow flowers, so I cut them off. Then last year I lost the senecio and I lost my rue. It was *indispensable*. I had big bushes of it here and there through this border. And I lost my santolinas, *all of them*, and lavenders. But the rue with its memories was the saddest loss of all. So I'm starting all over again."

Pam stopped and commented on another composition.

"This has got overgrown. I mean, that's the trouble, isn't it? Twenty years, thirty years on, I had to take the hedge out. It was dying all along this side where the shrubs had butted up against it. And I'm starting all over again from scratch. But in a way, that's the fun, you know—improvising."

To many people, green is green. Just that. Pam's eye seeks out all the infinite subtleties and variations in the colour. She pointed to a trio, a sweet synchrony

Pam Frost says, "This has got overgrown."

A serendipitous bouquet of variegation.

of variegated foliage ("clean and clearly defined") where the flowers of the poached egg plant (*Limnanthes douglasii*) poke through *Hosta* 'El Niño'.

"*Very* serendipitous, that is. Matter of fact, it happened once before with another hosta and I thought I'd like to try to create that again. The first time there was a blue geranium too. *Entirely unplanned.*"

What is Pam's idea of the perfect garden? She gives this some thought.

"First, Helen Dillon's garden in Ireland, which has a combination of all the most yummy plants and things you've never come across before, plus they're put together really, *really* well. Then Kathy Leishman's on Bowen Island is a lovely, inspiring garden."

Does she have any ambitions yet to fulfill as a gardener?

"Well, not *specifically*. I'd just like to keep on gardening as long as I possibly can. Next year is going to be *better*. I have a wonderful helper with pruning and

Pam Frost. "I love gardening. It's my life."

projects and things I can't manage on my own. We bounce ideas off each other, and it is all so invigorating."

Pam, like many gardeners, looks forward to a life annually refreshed with hope and expectation. "There's always next year. There'll be something you're going to see that you didn't see this year." She laughs happily. "I love gardening. It's my life. I'd like to be carried out of here feet first!"

David Goatley, portrait of artist and conservationist Robert Bateman, 1995, oil on canvas, 16 x 20 inches.

SIX

Making Pleasing Places

"I CAN'T CONCEIVE OF ANYTHING being more varied and rich and handsome than the planet Earth. And its crowning beauty is the natural world. I want to soak it up, to understand it as well as I can, and to absorb it . . . and then I'd like to put it together and express it in my painting. This is the way I want to dedicate my life."

Thus, Robert Bateman introduces his website. And he lives by those words.

As a wildlife artist, naturalist, environmentalist, and conservationist, Robert is famous. Twelve Canadian and American universities have bestowed honorary degrees on him. Three schools in Canada are named for him. The list of major awards and exhibitions, commissions, books, and films fills several pages. Less known is his artistry in creating the private outdoor spaces with which he and his wife, Birgit, have surrounded their home on Salt Spring Island. Indeed, it is an inspired space—part garden, part cultural museum, part architecture, all design—a place of wood and light, designed by the Batemans with their son-in-law, Rob Barnard, a disciple of Hank Schubart, who was a student of Frank Lloyd Wright.

"I've always been very, very attentive to *place*, to the feeling of a place," says Robert. "In fact, I have a lecture I give called 'Making Pleasing Places.' Most cultures try to make their places pleasing—except North American commercial culture, which aims to make instant pudding: sweet and slick, convenient, and replaceable next year.

"My sense of place is to work with nature, but unlike the great Canadian landscape architect Cornelia Oberlander, who tries to be all native, in working with nature I'm not trying to be a purist—Cornelia, by the way, helped Birgit with her homework when she had just arrived in Vancouver in 1955 and spoke no English. Part of my expression is reflecting the memory of my life in all the other places I've been and loved. That would include Japan and Europe among others. And the other thing (which really brings out my regard for Frank Lloyd Wright) is I'm *anti*-antebellum. You know, 'Ta-da, here it is'—the style where one's wealth is all hanging out at once? No, that's not for us. I want it to be discreet. I want it to be *discovered*. So here, in this place, you sort of twinkle through, and you're led along different pathways, coming across touches of Japan, Indonesia, hidden surprises, new discoveries as you go. That's part of the atmosphere.

Right: Before entering the garden, the fence and woodshed are intentionally placed to shut out the view.

Below: At the entrance, a Japanese-style lantern welcomes the visitor.

"To me, gardens are not just a whole bunch of plants. They're also about garden architecture. As a young man, I read *Down the Garden Path*, by Beverley Nichols, and I particularly remember one thing he said. 'No matter how

small your space is, you should always divide it into two parts, so that when you're in one part, you always have to go round a corner to discover what's in the other.' And in fact I divide our space into many different parts."

The lych-gate.

Indeed, discovering the Bateman place is analogous to the dance of the seven veils. New and delectable bits are revealed as you stroll.

"So as you drove in here, I didn't permit you to see the lake, which is one of the most charming features, or the old farmhouse, which dates from 1930, the year I was born. In spring it's all apple blossom. We bought forty acres here in 1987, and added another forty much later, but didn't build our house and move here till seven years ago. Meantime, that farmhouse has become part of our heritage. Most of our kids have lived there. Our granddaughter Annie was born there on the floor, with a midwife attending. And when you're in there with Annie and you ask her, 'Annie, where were you born?' she points and says, 'Right there!' She knows the exact spot.

"That bit of fence and the wood pile are intentionally placed, so I don't let you see the house as you pull up. Once you park and get out of the car, I try to make it clear where you're supposed to go."

Clear it was. There was only one way to go. We were funnelled toward the entrance along a short gravel pathway, fringed on the left with native ferns, Oregon grape, and mosses. To the right stands a welcoming lantern, which Robert designed, based on those at Ise, Japan's most sacred Shinto shrine. On both sides of the path, in homage to his native land and the provinces he has called home, he has planted five species of maple: the red maple (*Acer rubrum*) and sugar maple (*A. saccharum*) from Ontario, and the Douglas, vine, and bigleaf maples (*A. glabrum*, *A. circinatum*, and *A. macrophyllum*) from BC.

The pathway leads to the roofed lych-gate (a traditional entryway to English country churchyards), decorated inside and out with carvings and panels that, for Robert, carry some memory, some history.

Top: Descending toward the house, the overhead trellis helps conceal what lies beyond.

Right: Cookies or the real thing?

"Overhead, along the roofline there, you can see the diamond and oval pattern, which I call the Bateman theme. That was carved by our son John. As you'll see later, it relates to our front door, which I bought in Nigeria before we had our first house. There are also influences of Japan here, and Norse. Then, just to the left of the gate, that carved panel may be a couple of hundred years old. It comes from Lamu Island, an ancient Swahili-speaking Arab settlement just off the coast of Kenya."

The distance from the gate to the front door is only about fifty metres. But the journey crosses continents and spans cultures.

Robert opened the gate and a veil was removed. We stood at the top of a gently curving staircase: wide, concrete steps, swept clean but for a foraging patrol of small black ants crossing in single file from one side to the other. The curve conceals the bottom of the staircase. A discovery-in-waiting.

Water trickles from a wooden spout and drips onto a large stone.

"This is a combination of Bavaria and Kyoto. We lived in Bavaria for a year in an eighteenth-century farmhouse, and they had something like this, water spouting from a spring into a cattle trough. The carving is Bavarian in style, but the stone and the soft sound of water is reminiscent of what you might find in the garden of a Kyoto temple. This morning, when I got up to check things out, there was a little flock of siskins drinking there."

Below the water spout, descending as the steps descend, is a native garden of rock, moss, and familiar west coast plants such as shore pine, salal, ferns, Oregon oxalis, and kinnikinnick—an outcrop just as nature made it. Or so it appears.

But here, appearances deceive, because, as Robert declares, "Almost everything you see here is intentional, *contrived*. But, like the Japanese, I want to contrive it so it appears *not* to be contrived. Here I decided to create a pseudo-hilltop, as you might find on Salt Spring Island. So I went to the museum in Victoria and took a look at the west coast scenic diorama they had created there. There was no glass, and when the guard wasn't looking, I tapped on the rock, which looked totally real but in fact was hollow. So I phoned the museum and asked, 'How did you make those rocks?' And they said, 'Well, you get latex casting compound and cheesecloth, and you make a mould of a

piece of cliff that you like. Then you peel that off, line it with chicken wire, pour in a thin layer of cement and let it dry.' In this way you get what I call a 'cookie'—a replica in cement of the original cliff, about an inch and a half thick with chicken wire hanging out the sides. Then you can wire the cookies together and mortar in between, like building a gingerbread house. So this is a mixture of cookies and real rock, and after a time, the moss and lichen take hold and you can't tell the difference.

"We did have an excavator bring in some large rocks, but it's the cookies that tie them together. So, in your imagination, from the water source at the top a stream flows down this hill and into the dried-up stream beds lower down, though in fact, the water goes nowhere. It falls off the Kyoto stone into a concealed container and is recycled by a little pump."

"I don't want you to see too much."

An overhead trellis, a lattice, light and airy in structure, partly shades the staircase and once again, as Robert explains, creates a partial sight barrier, a veil, a bit of a mystery about what may lie beyond.

"I don't want you to see too much," he says.

"I've always loved trellises. In nineteenth-century Germany, mad King Ludwig—I must be rather like him—built a palace at Linderhof and there are wonderful arbours and trellises, all festooned with vines. I've also admired overhead open wooden structures in Africa, India, and Japan. And I want to bring fragrance into the air, so there's scented honeysuckle starting to weave through the lattice, and on the wall here, at nose level, there's lily-of-the-valley, which

always makes me think of my mother because they always bloomed on Mother's Day, when I would go into the garden and pick her a little bouquet. Like the whole garden, this is a work in progress."

At the foot of the stairs, a sensor detected our approach and threw light on a welcoming cedar pole, mounted on a wall. It was carved by Norman Tait, a Coast Nisga'a artist born on the lower Nass River.

"Back in the early 1980s, before we moved to the coast, just after my first show at the Museum of Vancouver, Norman brought this to the Museum of Vancouver store to sell. The woman who ran the store sent me a photograph and offered to hold it for me. I could see at once it was an exceptional piece. I think that most contemporary attempts at working in this tradition fall short, but here the form is full of movement. Everything is swelling or shrinking. 'We'll take it,' I said."

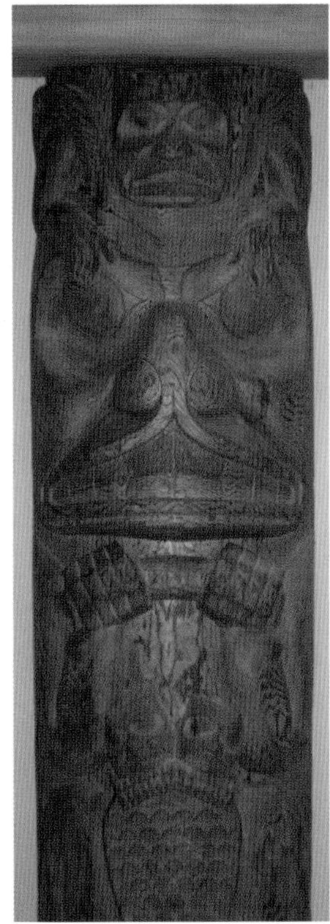

Above: First glimpse of the walled courtyard.

Left: A welcoming pole, carved by Norman Tait.

Within the courtyard.

At this point, the path takes a sharp turn, following the wall of the house. There are no windows for a peek inside. But on the left, the way is bordered by a waist-high wall, topped with short, peeled-cedar pillars.

"With these short posts, I've drawn little tableaux for you and framed them. They could be paintings. Or photographs—because when you frame the picture in the lens, you are defining the scene for the viewer. So it is here. Everything is framed, intentionally, enclosing a composition of natural-looking, mostly native plants and mossy rock—though once again, of course, these apparently uncontrived effects are entirely contrived."

The pool is the centrepiece of the courtyard and a safe home for the koi.

This remarkable journey from the gate to the front door ended with the final veil flung aside as we stepped into the sunlight and the serenity of the enclosed courtyard. Here, there's more than a hint of the *tsuboniwa*, the Japanese walled courtyard garden, especially in the stucco walls, topped with cedar, that frame two sides. Of course, these walls are not simply ornamental. They keep the deer out.

Within the courtyard, once again this part of the garden follows the contours of a rock-strewn hill: a mountain landscape in miniature. In winter, a spring-fed stream tumbles down, purling through a meadow, splashing over a small cliff into a pond—the central attraction of the courtyard. In summer, the stream is dry, and a pump creates the water flow. It's all *contrivance*.

Robert describes building this landscape with the aid of an excavator, placing the huge rocks that stabilize the foot of the hill and provide the foundation for the cliff—faced with cookies again, for surface texture. He deliberately left a little gap at the edge of a cookie, exposing the wire mesh, demonstrating the artifice.

He laughs. "As an artist, basically my whole life is faking nature!"

In designing the pond, Robert considered sanctuary for its residents. "The water goes way back beneath the paving stones where we're standing, and under here I've created apartment houses for the koi, so they can escape. That's where they hibernate in winter. The water's too deep for herons and raccoons, and I made sure the apartment doors were too small for otters to break in. But I didn't think of mink! We had forty koi at one point, until Birgit and I came back one day after our walk and found the mink had invaded and massacred all but five. We found one still alive over by the garage. Birgit grabbed it and slid it back into the water and it survived! So we set a live trap and caught two mink, then released them on a beach, miles from here. And thankfully, they haven't been back."

A third side of the courtyard is enclosed by the path we have travelled and a plain stucco wall, background for a bonsai mountain pine (*Pinus mugo*) in a black stoneware pot, a contemporary frog mask by the Haida artist Robert Davidson, and a beautiful Northwest coast ceremonial potlatch bowl, containing four green glass balls, long ago used to float the nets of Japanese fishermen.

The front door, inspiration for "the Bateman theme."

The house is entered from the fourth side of the courtyard. Small-paned windows in the French doors reflect the courtyard and allow a partial view through to the other side of the house—and more discoveries-in-waiting. To the left of the doorway, in a pocket of soil, a honeysuckle (*Lonicera japonica* 'Halliana') scrambles above a weeping Japanese maple and a moss-draped rock (this one is real).

Then, finally, the front door from Nigeria, the one that inspired "the Bateman theme" pattern of diamonds and ovals. Robert ran his hand across the heavily textured, glowing surface.

"This comes from the Awka region of the country. It's based on the doors to a chief's compound and made from a single plank of mahogany. Somewhere, there's just one small knot. I bought it in the mid-1960s, when I was teaching high school in Nigeria, and later had it installed in our house in Ontario. So it's part of our heritage now. This is its third and final home."

Beside this door, the theme is echoed in another work of tribal art from Awka, another solid mahogany door, mounted between poles. As with many of the architectural touches we have seen, Robert credits his son-in-law, Rob Barnard, with its elegant installation.

BIRGIT FREYBE BATEMAN is also an artist. A photographer, her work has appeared in books and magazines. It has been exhibited in galleries in North America and, most recently, at the Stroganoff Palace of the Russian State Museum in St. Petersburg, in the summer of 2011. In the introduction to the catalogue of that show, titled *Mindful Vision*, the museum's deputy director wrote, "Unexpected angles, attention to colour, and especially texture, are the characteristics typical of her work."

Birgit Freybe Bateman's *Frozen Grasses with Ice Patterns*. This image, captured at the edge of Ford Lake in front of Robert and Birgit's house, was included in the St. Petersburg Exhibition, 2011.

Yes, Birgit has a great eye for colour: at a street market in Sichuan, a child with yellow ribbons in her hair, wrapped in a sweater knitted with leftover wool of many colours; at a dusty market in Rajasthan, women clothed in saris and head scarves of many soft shades. These and many of her arresting images can be browsed on her website.

"I'm basically a photojournalist. I shoot on the fly," Birgit says. "You're walking past something that catches your eye, and you take it. And I've had a lot of really good luck with that."

"*Nothing* escapes her eye," Robert adds, "but it's the *aha!* moment that causes the artist in her to pause and take the shot."

"In photography, I do like just black and white," Birgit says, "but then I

Above: Birgit Freybe Bateman, photographer and gardener.

Above right: Birgit's passion for colour is displayed in her choice of plants. PHOTO BIRGIT FREYBE BATEMAN

think, 'Well, I love colour. How could I do just black and white?' Colour is so sensuous to me, so rich."

On the terrace in front of the house—the lake side—she had laid out tea, with fresh berries from the garden. Her love of colour was displayed in the bowl of sweet peas, the blue Royal Copenhagen china set, her vermilion shirt.

Robert observes, "I happen to have a passion for vermilion. As in the Grenadier Guards, or in geraniums galore, all over Switzerland and Austria, in all the window boxes and so on. I don't want magenta geraniums. I want mine to be vermilion. But on the whole, colour is not a thing which interests me as much as it does Birgit. I do have opinions on colour, and they coincide with hers. This flower border that runs the length of the terrace is rich in colour, and primarily her domain."

In the garden, the Batemans work together, though not elbow to elbow.

"With any idea he gets—and often it'll be him saying, 'We've got to have an impressive gate,' and I'll say, 'But not *too* impressive,' because I like things to look a bit humbler—the fabulous thing about Bob is that first of all, he *wants* my opinion, and second, he really does listen. We debate things back and forth, and sometimes he gets what he wants and other times I do. When it comes to spacing, both of us will agree, for example, that we want an area to look Asian, like having the Japanese maples up against the house. But

Robert's structures, Birgit's flowers.

they have already become too big. So when it comes to plants, I'm the reality check. I'll say, 'That's going to become out of scale,' and he'll say, 'Well, we can prune it.' And I'll say, 'Well, Bob, when you're gone, I don't want to have to keep paying for pruning!'

"I generally get the last word on plant choices. In front here, this border is constantly in flux. I love to grow plants that self-seed, like those little blue campanulas by the steps. Also, the native monkey-flower there, the mimulus. We both like a mix of nature doing its own thing, with us directing it ever so slightly. These nasturtiums were self-seeded—nature did that—but I picked all the large leaves, so the sun got in and we had more flowers, which I use in salads for colour and flavour.

"I love to come out first thing in the morning with my coffee, and just walk across this terrace, observing everything, picking a few weeds here and there, making decisions. Nothing gives me greater pleasure."

In front of the house, with a panoramic view of Ford Lake and the hills beyond, the foreground is filled with an eclectic mixed border, mainly perennial, giving expression to Birgit's passion for colour. The architecture here—trellises, gates, fencing—displays Robert's fancy, while Birgit's is applied to the choice and placing of plants, considering, above all, colour.

"The colours—what should go where? How to blend the lavender and roses,

The view from the terrace, in front of the house.

the lupins, pelargoniums, and petunias? For example, here we have the red cardinal flower, which will bloom a little later, accenting the coneflowers, echinacea. I like that combination. And I love all those bumblebees there. So nice! And that *Lychnis coronaria*, the rose campion, that's a surprise because it's white. Self-seeded too. And then, of course, fragrance is really important to me. Oh yes!"

AS THE BATEMANS walked us back to our car—through the house, savouring once again the peace of the courtyard, the sounds of birds and water, the artifacts of many cultures, the curving staircase, the lych-gate—Robert summarized his aesthetic.

"I like to integrate history and geography and biology and heritage and perhaps some modern aspects, all hanging together. I mean, some places I enjoy (like the Guggenheim Museum), are just modernist in style, while others (like Versailles), are seventeenth, eighteenth century in style. But mine is all over the

Birgit's blending of colour, fragrance, and surprise.

place. I remember when I was planning our first house, I would tell people, 'The effect I want is a kind of Japanesey/African/Spanish colonial/Tudor sort of look.' And people went, 'Aaargh—that's got to be the most horrible mishmash!' Then a friend who taught at the University of Toronto School of Architecture said, 'No, no, I wouldn't call it a mishmash. There's one word that would take in your taste and the word would be *peasant*.'

"I want it to look as if it's organic and living, and even if it's wood, each piece bears memory of a living thing. Or, even though the patio blocks are made of cement, an industrial product, there's moss growing in it, which I absolutely welcome. Then, the pots are made of clay, with glazes that are often organic in origin, and of course you get the plants growing in them and among them. So all this is integrated in what I love. I really, really like wilderness, but what I *especially* like is what you might call bucolic, or picturesque—where the hand of man has a gentle interface with nature.

"I like what Frank Lloyd Wright tried to do in his places. As you move through, you have an adventure in space, like moving through a piece of sculpture. You're closed in, then you open up, then you're closed in again, and things are framed. You're not just going from one box to another. That's what I think about making pleasing places."

The entry gate is itself a work of art.

SEVEN

A Garden Is a Poem

An armed sentry guards the poets' home.

"GARDENS ARE METAPHORS FOR WHO we were, are and will be. So, what should a gardener pay attention to? . . . Rhythm is important. A plant must be allowed its natural spread. Space is never empty in a garden. There is always something beyond for the eye to rest upon. The eyes shift from foreground to background. They take pleasure in the variations of depth, in the levels varying heights offer. A natural rhythm . . ."[1]

Through a delicate arched gate of thin wooden slats, glimpses of green, flashes of colour, the sound of water, and the promise of a secret, mysterious landscape just beyond. Open the gate and behold the garden world of Patrick Lane and Lorna Crozier, two of Canada's best-loved poets and writers of fiction, essays, and memoir. Their home and garden occupy about an acre of lush, flat land on a spacious but otherwise unassuming road on the Saanich Peninsula, north of Victoria, BC.

Step inside, to be confronted by a life-sized replica of a terracotta Xian warrior, standing sentry in an alcove and guarding the house and garden, a weapon clutched in each hand. Look more closely and notice that each clay hand shelters the body of a dead hummingbird, tiny casualties of attacking their reflections.

Patrick and Lorna moved to this property in 2005, to a mature garden with a decidedly Asian design and architecture. Though constantly reconsidering, refining, and lightly reconfiguring the space, they have maintained the

Top left: The garden world of Patrick Lane and Lorna Crozier.

Top right: Rock, water, and moss form the foundations of the garden.

original plan of the garden while adding objects and touches of imagination uniquely their own. Their gardening sensibilities spring from their geographical origins: Patrick from the British Columbia interior and north, Lorna from the Saskatchewan prairie. Their gardening perspectives are different, yet oddly compatible.

Patrick grew up in the Okanagan Valley, in the small town of Vernon.

"The natural garden is the world for me. I was extremely nearsighted as a child, almost blind, everything almost a complete blur. I had to imagine much of the world surrounding me, but I had no idea what was there. What I did see was everything very, very close up. I spent my time walking with my head down and I still do that. I'd look at what was right in front of my feet because I didn't want to trip and fall.

"On the other hand, Lorna sees everything, because she grew up on the prairie, where there are no impediments. For her, everything is vast distance and horizon. Here, she'd trip over a pebble because she's not looking at where she's walking. But then, there's nothing to trip over on the prairie. I grew up in a valley; Lorna grew up on a continent.

"So, we're perfectly suited to one another. I'll say, 'Look at that tiny beetle by the stone.' And Lorna will say, 'Isn't that fascinating, but look at those geese flying overhead.' I won't have noticed them. We see these two worlds together all the time, and it's the same in the garden."

As you enter their garden, your eye is drawn into a landscape of heights, textures, layers of foliage, and bursts of colour. Foreground and background are given equal regard. Sculptural rock formations rise from the ground naturally. A magnificent slate bench obligingly harbours small mounds of moss. Two graceful metal cranes engage in intimate conversation at the border of a bamboo grove. The narrow, meandering stream falling into a large pond is home to a healthy population of goldfish. Patrick muses that the scattered fish "are the water's thoughts." Two turtles are also in residence. The banks of the pond are undulating pillows of bright, glorious, green Irish moss, dotted with tiny white flowers. Patrick says that since moving to this house, he has had to learn the lore of mosses.

"Actually, this isn't a true moss at all; it's a flowering plant with roots and you have to fertilize it and look after it, which I didn't know at first. After we'd been here a few years, it started to show big brown spots. Lorna was very upset;

"The water's thoughts."

Between banks of Irish moss, water falls into the pool.

she thought it was dying. So this spring I fertilized it and boom!—after five years of neglect it became bountiful. Those white flowers have been blooming since late May, and here it's September and those billows are still awash with blossom. At one time, there were as many bees on it as there were flowers."

Because of his poor eyesight as a child, Patrick says he quickly came to appreciate the detail, "the intimacies," he calls them, of the living world.

"I delighted in feeding spiders, and became fascinated by the minuscule world of predators and prey. I didn't see the bears, moose, and deer. I saw the world down below. I was never happier than on my hands and knees on a hillside somewhere, poring over rocks and lifting them to find the tiny world underneath. I became intimately involved with the lichens, mosses, and grasses, the textures and fabric of tree bark. I didn't develop a sense of the larger display. Lorna is much better at seeing the grander order of the garden. She sees the complex display; I see the small, intimate moments."

Lorna remembers her husband introducing her to the drama of nature's intimate moments. "Patrick's favourite creature is the spider. When we first got together, he would take me to a web and say, 'Lorna, watch this. The little male spider is approaching a female. Look how delicately he walks the lines and how tentative he is and how she's waiting for him.' I wouldn't have discovered that on my own—not in those days. I was too busy."

She says that once she began sharing gardens with Patrick, her own interest in plants and gardens was refined and emphasized. "My mother and father were both farmers who lost the farm. When I was growing up, we rented houses in Swift Current, and the most important part of the lot was the vegetable garden. They never thought of beautifying the rest of the property; it would be full of crabgrass and they wouldn't have owned a mower. Dad collected oil drums and pipes and things in the yard, but the vegetable garden was always immaculate and central."

Lorna's early memories of planting start in the family potato patch, when she was four. "I remember, very, very fondly, planting potatoes with them. They didn't need me, but they included me. Dad would dig the hole, Mum would drop in the piece of potato with the eye, Dad would shovel earth on top, and it was my job to stamp. I felt so important walking those long rows stamping down the potatoes. We'd grow enough to last until the next spring, when they would plant again, using the ones left at the bottom of the bin as seed potatoes."

The intimate, naughty, sometimes risqué lives of vegetables are revealed in one of Lorna's best-known, much-loved, oft-quoted series of poems, *The Sex Lives of Vegetables*. Her carrots are priapic, the onion self-loving, hugging its layers. Lettuce is "a courtesan," cauliflower the garden's "pale brain," and so on. Consider the potato:

"Potatoes"

No one knows
what potatoes do.
Quiet and secretive
they stick together.
So many under one roof
there is talk of incest.

The pale, dumb faces,
the blank expressions.
Potato dumplings.
Potato pancakes.
Potato head.

In dark cellars
they reach across the potato bin
to hold one another
in their thin white arms.[2]

"That sequence originated from me just sitting out in the garden, thinking about the life of plants and what goes on in the garden when no one is there. I made it humorous by talking about their sex lives. But really, it was deeper than that in some ways. I gave them personalities, but I tried to remain true to what they were. It's a kind of meditation on the fact that no matter what we do there's growth, there's life, there's reproduction, and it's all taking place in a small plot.

"I made myself stick to the garden vegetables I was familiar with as a child. I didn't write about asparagus because we didn't have it. I wanted to be prairie-centric in approach to growth and life. I think for me what the garden has in common with writing poetry is that they are both timeless events. When I go into the garden, I can be there for three hours and have no idea how much time has passed. I feel the same way when writing a poem. Time disappears and it's me and the language and rhythm of it and the images.

To Patrick, this miniature Japanese maple is a poem.

When I'm in the garden, I get into the rhythm of weeding or digging and there's no sense of time. There's no ego in the garden. As with writing, you have to leave your ego behind. I love it because it's an act of creativity; it becomes very meditative and puts me in the kind of attentive state I have to be in for a poem to come."

Equally entranced by the garden's rhythm, Patrick expresses fulsome admiration for Lorna's popular vegetable poems. "Unbelievably, that book became a Canadian bestseller—an oxymoronic phrase when talking about poetry. I was both in awe and in envy. I was writing about some la-de-dah Persian image and I thought, 'Why am I not out in the garden writing about carrots?' Then I told myself, 'Patrick, centre yourself!' That's what we do for each other: we centre each other in simple things and that's what the garden offers us sometimes—a certain kind of simplicity."

The garden also offers an escape from language, Patrick says. "I'm like the unicorn in the fabulist world. I sit in my office, but have to get up regularly and ease my back. So I'll wander around the garden, observing things, maybe not doing much. If I remember to take a pair of secateurs, I'll prune a bit of *Pieris japonica* or whatever. The creative is never farther away than the things that surround us.

Wabi: silvery lichen ornaments an azalea.

"To me, that little bonsai there is a poem, an arrangement of stone, sand, moss, and tree—all in a harmonious, contained space. What else can a poem be but the same kind of contained space?"

We considered this point while Patrick grabbed his secateurs and crossed the garden to lop a shoot thrusting skyward from a deodar he has trained as a prostrate shrub. The deodar wants to be a tree. "That's better," he said, and he was right. Balance was restored.

In their garden the contained spaces, large and small, reflect their desire to see the architecture of certain trees and shrubs. A magnificent, prostrate maple, branches of an azalea frosted with lichen, a yew with exposed, python-like coiled and twisted limbs, and, by the front gate, a diseased cherry tree with moss-covered branches. Patrick reluctantly admits the tree should be taken out, but says, "I'll let it stay. It has such lovely white blossoms in the spring, and from time to time I hear a tree frog croaking there. As the Japanese say, 'It has a lot of *wabi*.' That means life and death combining in the same plant. Half of it is dying and new growth is coming too. Balance."

Evolving as a gardener, Patrick describes having to tame dual impulses: a desire for order and patience versus the thrill of acquiring more and more botanical treasures.

"Sometimes, with a kind of urgency—less planning and more impulse—interesting things occur. Hidden behind the main garden is where I've put the garden's extras—plants I've split off or bits and pieces from friends. It's really a hodgepodge, but in some ways it's a happier place than this area here, which is more ordered.

"But for me, the planned spaces in the garden are small tableaux, areas with small rooms, each with its own dramatic setting and certain plants to engage the senses. Like that small part of the garden over there with the bamboo, a

One of Patrick's favourites—a small room of shade plants.

very shady area with beautiful mosses, a variety of ferns, and other unusual species of shade plants. I get tremendous pleasure walking there, though it's only six or eight feet long by two feet wide. It doesn't get any sun, only mottled light, but everything there is extremely happy. It's a contained, tiny room with a very deliberate choice of plants."

Every gardener struggles with the desire to create order while nature wishes to go its own way. Patrick and Lorna are no different. She says that after living together in Saskatoon, where the prairie climate tests and limits the gardener's desires, she and Patrick were greedy when they settled on the BC coast.

"We bought every beautiful shrub, bush, plant that wouldn't grow in Saskatchewan or even in the Okanagan when Patrick was a boy. We planted them en masse and within a couple of years, they'd grown huge. There were at least twice as many shrubs as there should have been. On the prairies, they would have worked; they would have taken twenty years to achieve growth

Anenome hupehensis.

and height in appropriate arrangement, and they would have been lovely. Here, you're always cutting back. You can't be a gardener here without a half-ton truck to haul stuff to the dump. Our compost bins aren't big enough."

Patrick agrees. "As I've grown older and been a gardener longer, I've discovered the laws of proportion and have recognized that some plants will occupy a given space and are content with that. I've learned to find the proportionate balances amongst plants because in my early gardens, I really didn't give much thought to that; I had no sense that individual plants would increase in volume and size and create disproportion, imbalance. They offend nature; they disturb the harmonies that could occur. You seldom find false harmony in nature.

"We labour to create an ordered world and the garden insists on being itself. And it will have its way with you. You'll put plants in a certain place and they will promptly die. They have their own ideas of how and where they're supposed to survive. We've turned them into slaves in a way. In this garden, things are constantly being contained and controlled and reduced, and all the plants are struggling against the impetus I have to keep them in the structure designed for them. Nature is tolerating me—to a degree."

In another poem, Lorna describes the will of the garden.

"In Moonlight"

Something moves
just beyond the mind's
clumsy fingers.

It has to do with seeds.
The earth's insomnia.
The garden going on
without us

needing no one
to watch it

not even the moon.[3]

IT'S HARDLY SURPRISING that when Lorna and Patrick were looking for a garden and property with more light, they chose this established, Asian-style garden. Patrick, particularly, has long been attracted to the simplicity of traditional Japanese horticulture—sensibilities so evident in this garden.

"One of the more blessed times in my adult life was when I was in Japan and took some extra time and visited the gardens of Kyoto. Blissful, the quiet. We struggle to make everything instantly perfect in the garden, forgetting that the laws of the natural world require some time to establish—maybe two or three hundred years. We're so impatient now: you watch a house going up and next thing you know the property also includes a completed garden—fully grown trees, shrubs. That urgency sacrifices the joy of growing, changing—the garden's serendipity. Take these tiny maples here, for instance. They're volunteers, and when they were just seedlings, rather than pull them up, I dug them up, replanted them and have been nurturing them ever since. I could have gone and bought a bonsai, or searched in the hills to find a mature tree that had been suffering terribly for fifty years so that it was all contorted. But to take those seedlings and raise them, for me, it was giving them life but also creating a slight, intimate drama of the tree, which is very much the concept of bonsai."

Lorna feels that her husband's passion for these spare, simple miniatures contrasts with the burgeoning beds in the larger garden. She says she craves space.

Lorna Crozier and Patrick Lane; tea in the *machiya*.

"Patrick joked about my obsession with our former garden. He says that every year I insisted that at least one tree be cut down. Eventually, he said, our garden would be a wheat field. I could certainly do with fewer trees because a garden, for me, is also a space that holds the light. It's a receptacle for what's above it, for the sky. I get very unhappy when I can't see the sky. When we found this property, I loved that it's open enough for me to stand and still feel the air around me and that the landscape isn't moving in on me. I'm only happy when I have that open feeling, when the sun is shining and I can walk out and into it. I don't want the garden to feel like a forest."

Patrick, now in his early seventies, says this will be his last garden.

"After this, I'll be a demented old man living in a small room. Lorna, I hope, will still be there with me. But even then I'd have a garden. As long as there's a window with light coming through, I'd have a little bonsai tree. A small, hollowed-out rock, a bit of volcanic pumice stone, a tree, and a bit of moss. That's a full garden. You can make a garden in a thimble."

As Patrick writes in his memoir, "Done well, a garden is a poem, and the old lesson of gardening is the same in poetry: what is *not* there is just as important as what is."[4]

David and George Lewis.

EIGHT

Still Dreaming of Paradise

IT IS OFTEN SAID THAT the gardener's desire to arrange the ground and make it bloom is deeply driven by a primal quest for paradise. George Little and David Lewis embarked on that quest separately, fuelled by early, inspirational, indelible memories—the lush, tropical setting of the musical *South Pacific* (Little) and a fourteen-year-old boy's joy in discovering Greek and, later, Egyptian antiquity (Lewis). Today, they are gardeners, artists, and partners. They are also celebrities—famous for their small, brilliantly colourful garden on Bainbridge Island, a thirty-five-minute ferry trip from downtown Seattle. Though George has now legally changed his name from Little to Lewis, Bainbridge Islanders, gardeners, and fans throughout the Pacific Northwest know them as Little and Lewis. Like Rodgers and Hammerstein, first names are not necessary.

"The girls."

For George and David, their garden story is their love story. They happily shared both with us on a cool, sunny day in late July, having recently hosted more than fifteen hundred people visiting the garden on the annual Bainbridge in Bloom tour. As we walked up the drive, a raucous serenade of hens greeted us. Even the henhouse bears singular Little and Lewis touches of colour and design, and as we were shown around, the occupants loudly boasted of their egg-laying efforts.

The property is just under a third of an acre, about half of which is the front garden, an arresting array of plants, many in pots. Exotic colour in both bloom and large-leaved foliage pervades, with a playful eye to arrangement. There are countless dense and wonderful views to be found. Looking through the leaves,

Above: Lush and tropical elements are playfully assembled.

Opposite: The trademark Little and Lewis blend of colour, foliage, and artwork.

fronds, or grasses in the foreground of any bed, the eye is lured by splashes of colour and different textures in the background. George recalls the origin of his love of the exotic in the garden.

"What got me interested in tropicals was seeing *South Pacific* as a child. I totally fell in love with that vegetation, everything tropical. And then, in a magazine of my mother's, I saw a beautiful column with things growing out of it. I later learned it was the design of the architect Antoni Gaudí, probably for a structure in the Park Güell in Barcelona. It fascinated me, and for years I wondered, 'How could I make something like that?'"

In their garden, casually interspersed among the plantings, are the daring and delightful sculptural objects that are unmistakably pure Little and Lewis. Vivid, azure-washed terracotta columns support a trellis, while others of differing heights are topped with delicately tinted concrete leaf sculptures or pots containing blooming masses. Glazed pots of blue and green, natural concrete or weathered terracotta are arranged in clusters, some on pieces of column, some containing water gardens. Giant, glossy pomegranates nestle among bamboo groves or the chocolate and scarlet leaves of taro.

The raintree.

Dominating a central pond is a signature Little and Lewis creation—the "raintree," a moss-covered, conically shaped pillow on a concrete "trunk," dripping water softly and seductively into the pond at its feet. The whole picture is enchanting.

David starts by explaining that this is a new garden for them. "Our old garden, next door, became very well known, and we'd have between three and five thousand people visiting it over the course of a summer. Three and half years ago, a couple came in, clients of ours, and the gentleman said in an offhand kind of way, 'If you ever think of selling this property, please give us first right of refusal.' Well, it took George and me about ten seconds to say, 'Make us an offer.' The offer was one we couldn't refuse, and they also let us stay there while we remodelled this small house here."

The new garden, though slightly smaller, did have its challenges.

"Three years ago, it was nothing more than a sloped, mossy lawn," David says.

"A tired, old, mossy lawn," adds George. "The house was built in 1963 and the only original growing thing we kept was this Japanese maple. Apparently, it's a variety brought over from Japan and planted in the mid-1960s in the Pacific Northwest. It has a growth habit like the thread-leaf variety, but with foliage like a regular maple leaf. We've never pruned that tree, just taken out dead branches. That open, undulating structure is the way it grows. Everything else that you see here is less than three years old."

"The first thing was to create a little bit of hardscape," says David. "We got rid of the grass, had the terrace laid and a pool made. George and I are very inspired by the archaeology of Greece and other ancient cultures, and the colours of Mexico reverberate in our garden. When I was fourteen, my father took our family to Crete for a year. We lived in a small fishing village, and that year changed my life. Absolutely changed my life. I discovered archaeology and have been fascinated with it ever since. Also, I fell in love with the landscape of Crete. There's an archaeological site there called Lato, a Doric site, where they used walls of boulders called Cyclopean walls—Cyclopean because the archaeologists can't imagine how such huge stones were manoeuvred into place except by giants. We love that look, and on a much smaller scale, our steps, pool, and other stonework are evocative of Lato."

Evocations of
ancient cultures.

By using bricks and stones to create beds, Little and Lewis can move, change, and create planting spaces at will. David explains, "In all of our gardens, we follow two fundamental rules. First, there are no plans. We've never had a plan. We just wake up in the morning, perhaps begin to carve out an area, and then arrange some pots or plant something new in it. That's how we garden."

George adds, "One thing inspires something else. We'll decide, 'Wouldn't it be fun to have a fountain here?' then create a space. Basically, we just play."

David continues, "The second fundamental is water, which plays a critical role. Water is the lifeblood of any garden, of us ourselves. Water is literally the source of whatever else we do in this garden."

"It's a sacred element," George says. "Watching a fountain is like watching a

Top: Contorted branches of a Japanese maple embrace a gallery of wall sculptures.

Above: Tropical water lily 'Ultra Violet'.

fireplace. It's hypnotic. Gazing into a pond is pure tranquillity."

The mention of tranquillity set off a grand cackle of hens. With apologies, David interrupted the conversation. "You keep talking, George. I'm going to find out what's up with the girls."

Deconstructing the famous Little and Lewis drip fountains and raintrees, George acknowledges that he and David have carefully refined their techniques and designs over the years. "We did the one next door about fifteen years ago, prompted by my fascination with trees in the forest and mountain streams. I love it when a waterfall seeps down through the mosses, the sound of water and the look of the damp moss. So we put the two together—tree forms and dripping mosses—and it worked. I love it! It's a very simple fountain; it doesn't need much. That pool where the raintree stands is about ten feet in diameter but only about nine inches deep. We do round shapes, umbrella forms, mushroom shapes. Then we plant them with mosses, baby's tears, and also speedwell, with little blue flowers.

Above: Wire frames for raintrees.

Opposite: The colours of the tropics. Clockwise from top left: Peachy-pink *Abutilon* hybrid, scarlet *Begonia boliviensis*, Taro (*Colocassia esculenta* 'Black Magic'), yellow *Brugmansia* 'Charles Grimaldi'.

"A stream of water can become annoying in five minutes, besides driving everyone to the bathroom. But dripping water is relaxing and has a charmingly musical sound. The minute people walk into this garden, you can see their shoulders relax as they are captivated by the tranquil sound."

The hens, too, had relaxed. Each of "the girls" is named for a French pastry—tartine, brioche, etc. Appropriately and obligingly, their noisy interlude produced four eggs.

Coincidentally, it was a fountain that introduced David Lewis the neophyte gardener to George Little the sculptor. In the late 1980s, David purchased a George Little fountain and invited him over to see how he'd installed it. George insisted that David's pond should be larger, and they both dug in. Their friendship developed while sharing this and subsequent projects, and eventually they became partners in a new business designing and selling garden fountains, pools, and pond structures. Their reputation as garden sculptors and designers grew. So also did their respect and affection for each other develop and deepen, until their partnership became a shared life—house and garden and pets, including the aforementioned poultry and three lively dogs, Sadie, Filo, and Byron.

A giant ceramic tetrapanax leaf glows within this exotic array.

Now they share the studio work and also collaborate in the garden. David has assumed the managerial tasks necessary to the business, and thus leaves most of the planting and aesthetic decisions to George. In their book, *A Garden Gallery*, David describes their collaboration. "For two artists to work together on nearly everything is rare. We sign both our names to every piece that comes out of our studio. Our styles and interests are different, but the blend of our skills, personalities, and passions creates a single entity: Little and Lewis."[1]

While David and George rejoice in the solidity of Little and Lewis, they prefer to keep their garden on the move, fluid in design. David says, "One of the things George has taught me, as we've worked together all these years, is that nothing is permanent; everything can be changed. The use of pots and potted plants gives us freedom: if an arrangement isn't working, we can move the pots around and create different compositions, without a lot of effort. In fact, George's policy, the challenge he insists on every year, is that we arrange the pots in different configurations, change it up."

This collection of gems not only merits annual rearrangement, but the plants also need to be stored each winter in the greenhouse behind the house, particularly the adored potted tropicals. Though they might bemoan the physical labour of heaving huge pots around, Little and Lewis love the flexibility of design. "It's like paint," David says. "If you don't like the colour, change it.

Mammoth tusks erupt from the woodland floor.

The garden gallery of Little and Lewis: an ecstatic blending of art and nature.

We're fearless and playful, especially with this garden that is so intimate. It's not for anybody else but us."

The playful arrangement of playful objects is deftly achieved in this garden: scarlet pomegranates huge enough to feed a Cyclops loll about here or there; a life-sized concrete tetrapanax leaf washed in lime-green and orange nestles underneath a prehistoric tree fern; a dinosaur egg, its top sliced off, provides a cozy nest for a cluster of echeverias.

Erupting from a bed of hostas beneath the canopy is a small grove of terracotta-coloured concrete tusks. Like a new tooth, the sharp tip of another is busting through paving stones at the edge of the path. Bizarre but beautiful, the tusks look as though they belong: a visiting neighbour recently asked George, "Are they growing there?"

David defines another Little and Lewis impulse. "As artists, we love to take a form from nature, use it to inspire a permanent object, and then put it back into nature. A full circle of creation." George adds, "I also love mysterious detail. When I was young, I was given a copy of *The Secret Garden*, which became a holy book for me. I've always been captivated by the idea of a hidden or secret garden, contained and cloistered, with beautiful objects accompanying the plants. Every garden we create has secrets, and because there's no plan, we can invent new secrets. We're always tinkering; it's *never* perfect."

Little and Lewis rejoice in building and continuing to share their garden and their partnership. Though happily anticipating marriage sometime soon, David describes their life together as "a ménage à trois." He says, "There are three of us here—George, me, and the garden—working together to make it something wonderful."

George also treasures their shared pursuits of gardening and art. "I love learning from what you do while you're doing it. For me, I dream into my work; I dream into our pleasure in the garden. That's also how I approach painting—like a waking dream. As a friend once said to me, 'We garden because we remember paradise.'"

At Linda Cochran's garden gate, a Little and Lewis creation.

NINE

Brazen Beauty

IF GARDENS WERE SECTIONS OF a symphony orchestra, Linda Cochran's would be the brass. It is unabashedly bold, proclaiming her love of the exotic, of colour, of size.

Among her sources of inspiration, she acknowledges a debt to George Little and David Lewis, and indeed, some of their work has a place in her garden. The first piece we noticed, when we visited her Bainbridge Island garden in late July, was a terracotta-coloured concrete bullfrog guarding the garden gate, all the while blasting forth its bass-tuba mating call and croaking Linda's name for the place: "Froggy Bottom," a takeoff on the Washington, DC, district Foggy Bottom.

"Yes, Little and Lewis made it for me. However, they don't want to make any more. They fear that everybody who sees this would like to have one—so perhaps your readers should know that this is a one-off.

"Actually, there are a *lot* of frogs here," says Linda. "This part of the island is very moist. The natural soil doesn't drain very well. If you dig a hole you'll get a puddle. So the frogs like it down here, and in the spring, they give a choral concert every evening. There's a drainage ditch over there, which I've pretty well abandoned to the frogs. It's hard to keep a wetland weeded.

"Years ago, this used to be a military base. Part of it was a communications centre during World War II, and the probably apocryphal story is that it was here they intercepted the signals that led to the breaking of the Japanese code. There was a communications tower on this spot, and some twenty years ago when we were building, the excavators kept running into these great steel cables that had to be cut with welding torches. So who knows what's under the ground here? Whatever there is may explain why everything grows so big! We started from scratch. Everything you see, I planted."

THE LARGE MAIN garden is completely hidden behind an evergreen thicket, pierced by a short, leafy tunnel, at the end of which an ornamental iron gate shuts out the deer. A heron perched on the gate waits patiently for a fish that will never appear. From outside, there's only a tantalizing hint of what lies beyond—a patch of sunlit lawn, scarlet blooms of *Crocosmia* 'Lucifer'. We were eager to ask the sentry frog to stand aside and let us into this beckoning space, but first, said Linda, we must see the large border that screens the house from the roadway.

"I decided that this area outside the gate had to be totally drought-tolerant, and deer-resistant too; we get a lot of deer wandering all over the island. I sort of took my cue from Beth Chatto's gravel garden. I never water this bed. I want it all to look kind of wild, as if it put itself there."

In this bed, Linda's palette is grey-blue and grey-green, with splashes of brighter green, silver, yellow, and red. The display is anchored by a grove of

Linda Cochran doesn't hesitate to reveal the virtues of weeds, such as Scots thistle, here seizing space between a restio and the scarlet spikes of *Lobelia tupa*.

Above left: Linda's palette of metallic greys, blues, and greens.

Above right: Beyond this ornamental gate lies Linda's "special world."

eucalyptus trees thought to have been killed by a sudden and severe November frost two years earlier, until they reappeared in more shrubby form, as often happens with eucalypts. These fill the background with fresh grey-blue foliage. The Scots thistle, with its large spiny leaves, is given full rein. Linda confessed that this biennial is on the noxious-weeds list in Washington State.

"I don't think it's a Class One weed. You're allowed to have it in the garden, but nurseries aren't allowed to sell it. However, I did have a visit from the authorities once, after a garden tour. Somebody ratted on me! That was for heracleum, the giant hogweed. It's gone now."

Here, Linda has redefined the meaning of weed (which is, after all, simply a plant in the wrong place). The Scots thistles joyfully mix in carefree abandon with other self-sown "weeds," such as the towering yellow spikes of the common mullein and the annual pink opium poppies, as well as with plants generally considered more garden-worthy, such as the Australian bottlebrush shrub, cardoon (the artichoke thistle), and different species of steely-grey-blue eryngium. There's a *Nolina* 'La siberica', a yucca relative from Mexico. It has flowered earlier, and the towering stem stands as a reminder. There are rosettes of the lancelike leaves of echium ("If they ever bloom, that will be a spectacular sight, with their ten-foot spikes") and, growing among them, tall *Lobelia tupa*, from central Chile.

"I have the lobelia all over the place, because the hummingbirds like it so much and it gives them something at this time of the year. Other birds, too, love this area. It's full of seed for them. Earlier in the year, I had a lot of *Eremurus robustus* in here, the foxtail lilies."

We could imagine their flowering spires, a stately attraction very much in keeping with this festive array.

Linda proudly showed us something we had never seen in cultivation in the Pacific Northwest: a *Restio rhodocoma capensis*, a plant endemic to the *fynbos*, the Cape Floral Kingdom, south of Cape Town.

"When I first got it, they weren't common here at all. People didn't know how to plant them. And I don't think anyone realized how big they get. But I like *size*. I don't go in for those dainty little rock garden plants, though some of them are quite nice. Certainly out in this location, anything small would be overwhelmed."

Top: *Restio rhodocoma capensis*.

Above: We visited too late to see this exuberant display of foxtail lilies. PHOTO LINDA COCHRAN

WE WALKED THROUGH the gate and into the sun-drenched main garden and the visual equivalent of a fanfare. After the relatively muted tones of the dry border, the impact of Linda's composition in size and colour is stunning. Wow!

"Yes, I do like colour. Shape is important too. I want it to look kind of tropical. So there are bananas. In a good year the leaves may grow eight feet or more. And now that I'm into photography, I'm looking for plants I can

Painting with plants.

photograph. I want flowers that fill the frame. I like colour a lot, and I like colour that's in the jewel tones. I don't like pastels particularly."

Linda has set aside the generally accepted rules of colour.

"There was a book by Myles Challis, *Exotic Gardening in Cool Climates*, about having a tropical-looking garden in a temperate climate. He was the one who got me started in this direction. Little and Lewis were certainly an influence, because they introduced me and a lot of the gardening world to the idea that it was good to have things in the garden that are painted in bright colours. Before that, people would have fountains or statuary that were classical in style, and the tasteful thing was to have a subdued palette. I remember reading that you should *never* have magenta with yellow and you should *never* have orange in your garden. Well, those are the colours I like! And you should never have red with pink, but I like red with pink! And of course, everyone should have a white garden and be like Sissinghurst. In my garden, you'll occasionally see white flowers, but I really don't like white. I would never plant a white garden.

"I thought about how Little and Lewis use colour, and I thought about the kind of art I like. Then, the more I got into photography, the more I thought about colour. So that now I have what, at least for me, is a good colour palette that makes other things look good: magentas, yellows, oranges, and blues. And they have to be saturated blues.

"Some people say they don't like yellow, but you *need* yellow. Yellow makes other things pop up, and you need orange too, for the same reason. You put them all together and it works, if you keep a rough parity between the pinks, the yellows, and the blues. Then green is the resting point. You know, people ask, 'If you don't have white in your garden, where is the eye going to rest?' And I say, 'On the green.'

In Linda's garden of startling colour, green provides a resting point for the eye.

Green in all shapes, shades, and sizes.

"The green is the background to everything in the garden. There are so many different kinds of green—silvery green, yellow green, blue green, grey green, lime green. Foliage may be shiny or matte, rough or smooth. Different shades, different shapes and sizes, different looks at different times of day. There's so much variation and yet, in all, green is a calm place to rest the eye. I used to have a lot of foliage colour in the garden. I used to buy every single variegated plant I could find, but now I'm getting away from that. I think it's better to have a lot of different textures and shades of green, especially if you have a lot of flower colour. It gives the eye something to rest upon."

Linda showed us around, her commentary full of delight and punctuated with merry laughter. First she turned to the sunny side of the thicket that borders the gate.

"I call this 'the clash of the Titans.' I love the way all these vines and climbers weave together and the different shapes and shades of green. There's the Chilean glory vine, *Eccremocarpus scaber*. There are hops, a hardy schefflera,

Top: "The clash of the Titans."

Above: *Trachycarpus fortunei.*

and the crimson glory vine, *Vitis coignetiae*, with the big, rounded leaves that turn crimson in fall."

Close to the "clash," Chusan palms add bold marks of exclamation.

"I've tried all sorts of palms, and I've decided that trachycarpus is the only one worth planting here. All of these I planted when they were small and had no trunks.

"I used to have a lot more grasses than I have now. I used to have every grass that was available. But after a while, I found they were kind of boring, especially the big pampas grasses. A lot of work, too. They were just a pain to deal with after the winter. The books say grasses provide winter interest, but not here where it rains so much. In winter they just sag, and the seed heads get wet and bedraggled and fall on the ground. They don't work here. But I still use grasses, smaller ones in soft lime green."

In a sunny bed, surrounded by lawn, Linda grows calla lilies, *Zantedeschia aethiopica*, most commonly seen in stark white, the easiest colour to grow. But disliking white, she has found lovely tones of orange and yellow that are far more subtle and engaging. In this flower, Linda shares the passion of the painter Georgia O'Keeffe, who depicted it so often and in such provocative ways that she became known as "the lady of the lilies."

"I got the orange one specifically to photograph it. That yellow one starts out quite pale, then gradually darkens and takes on a touch of pink, and if you look into the centre, the bottom of the bowl is a rich burgundy-wine colour."

Calla lilies.

In the same bed grows a patch of Iceland poppies. White is permitted, perhaps excused by the brilliant yellow centre of the flowers, which pose prettily for Linda's camera. With regular deadheading, she says, they've been blooming for months.

Complementing the calla lilies is the unfurling foliage of a banana (*Musa sikkimensis* 'Red Tiger'), with reddish stripes on the leaves.

"The more common hardy banana is *Musa basjoo*, but I much prefer this one. The leaves are *so* beautiful. I also have the Abyssinian banana, *Musa ensete*, with the dark underside to the leaves, but that's in a pot that I can move inside for winter, because it's much less hardy."

Opposite: The flair of Iceland poppies (*Papaver nudicaule*).

Above left: The Darjeeling banana (*Musa sikkimensis*).

Above right: The Abyssinian banana, with *Begonia boliviensis* 'Bonfire'.

LINDA AND HER husband, David Jurca, moved to Bainbridge Island in 1981, commuting by ferry to Seattle, where both worked as lawyers. Their first island house stood on a half-acre lot, and there Linda started her first garden. She had always wanted to garden. Her mother, who came from a farming family, inspired an early interest: Linda remembers how much she enjoyed poring over Wayside Gardens catalogues, helping her mother choose plants.

"I was always attracted to the idea of growing things, and I always wanted to be in a place where I could live on the land instead of going to a downtown office, working with lawyers yelling at each other. I find gardening very soothing. You know, if you're stressed out and get out in the garden, all the stress goes away.

"When I was lawyering—and that's a high-stress profession—for relaxation I would read gardening books. The good ones, in my opinion, were the English gardening books, because they looked at it in a very professional way and went into it in depth, whereas so many of the American ones just skimmed the surface. And when I looked at the Royal Horticultural Society's *Plant Finder* and all the plants that were available in Britain, it just made me drool!

"But for me, I think the major turning point was Heronswood, which Dan Hinkley was starting just as I was getting into gardening. By then, I had read all the English gardening books and learned about all those fabulous plants. But they weren't available here, at least not until Heronswood. For me it was a big impetus, and for many other gardeners too. I spent a lot of time over there. I used to give tours for Dan. And when it shut down, it was a shock for everybody.

"Then, when we moved into this house in '93, my daughter was three, and I decided that I'd give up lawyering and stay home with her—and garden! So that's what I've done.

"We moved to this house because I needed the space to have a Beth Chatto-style garden. This was ideal. There was no garden here and I had about an acre and a half to work with. I wanted it to be naturalistic, in that the beds kind of flow with the land. No straight lines. Chatto's book about gardening in boggy places, *The Damp Garden*, recommended using plants that are very lush and have big foliage. I kind of like that look, and this part of the island is very wet, so it lends itself to that kind of gardening. Then, when Chatto built her gravel garden and I saw pictures of it, I was really impressed. It was a different-looking garden to anything I'd seen before, so that's what I wanted to do out front."

LINDA LED US into the shady and moist woodland that borders the length of the lawn.

"It's about time I checked this out. I haven't been in here for quite a while. There's about an acre in here, and mostly I leave it alone."

Once again, in this well-mulched, rich soil, everything is supersized: gunnera leaves large enough to take a nap in; dinner plate-sized leaves of podophyllum (mayapple) and arisaemas (cobra lilies). Besides these, different greens, different shapes, ferns, black bamboo, clumps of persicaria, ground covers of lungwort, arum, and Oregon oxalis, and many, many other cool and relaxing sights. Some of these are invasive, but, left to work it out among themselves, they seem to have struck a truce. Weeds don't get much of a look-in. There's also an enormous ceramic pot with two bamboo poles poking out like giant chopsticks. The pot has a crack on one side, so water fills it only partway. And thereby hangs a tale.

"I was working in the garden one evening and just as it was getting dark, I heard what sounded like a baby crying. So I came out here and discovered a baby raccoon in this pot. Couldn't get out. The poor thing was whimpering and crying, just like a baby. So I got a bucket, pulled it out and put a blanket over it. And it didn't move, so I just left it alone, figuring its mother was around somewhere, and sure enough, in the morning it was gone. Well, I didn't want to come out one day and find a dead baby raccoon in here, so I put in these bamboo poles. It's my raccoon ladder!"

Throughout Linda's garden, enormous ceramic pots are placed and grouped with other artifacts and plants to compose still-life pictures. Some brim with rainwater. The surfaces, opaque with bright green algae, mirror the overhead foliage.

In the lawn stands a *Magnolia macrophylla*, the bigleaf magnolia, the largest in leaf and flower of all magnolias native to North America. Indeed, it has the largest leaves of *any* plant native to North America. Linda pointed out that its rapid upward growth has shaded out a previously sunny bed.

"I'm going to have to move those delphiniums. Instead I'm planning a spread of Himalayan blue poppies and lady's slipper orchids. What do you think?"

We thought the idea imaginative, innovative, ambitious, exotic.

"I do like my garden to look exotic. Bamboo gives it that look."

So do the bananas, the podophyllum, and the enormous leaves of the *Tetrapanax papyrifer* (used to make rice paper), with its long, peach-coloured stems. Behind the tetrapanax, a hefty clump of pale yellow Asiatic lilies, standing two metres tall or more, is starting to bloom. It seems her plants strive

Geranium 'Roxanne'.

to meet Linda's expectations for size, growing beyond their normal stature. Perhaps they sense her unhesitating readiness to get rid of anything that doesn't measure up.

"People have said this is a tropical-looking garden, but I don't want to be defined by that. When I enter the gate, I want to be in my own world, my own space. I'm away from everything else. And I want it to be a special world, and I don't want it to be too precious, but rather a private place that is somewhat exotic, a space that showcases those plants that I really like. If I really like a plant, I want to give it enough room to develop in the way it wants to develop. I don't plant too closely. And when I find the right place for a plant, I want it to develop in a way that it's either going to be a star or it's going to be supporting a star. I used to consider what other colours were beside it. But now I believe any colour will go with any other colour. I mean, if you pay too much attention to flower colour combinations, nature too often disappoints. They probably won't flower together even if you planned it that way. So why bother?

Above: The water mirrors the Chusan palm.

Below: Linda Cochran in her "special world."

"I think once you've established the structure, the framework, in the garden—the bamboos, the palms, the trees, the walls—and this garden's old enough now that it has structure, then the planting places can have pretty well anything in them. At one time, in building the framework, I tried to plant a hedge back there, and then I concluded that hedging is a bad thing, because if you have all of one plant, sooner or later one of them is gonna die, and then you've got a gap. So I hit upon bamboo. And now I think that's been very successful, a great way to create a backdrop, because there are a great many different kinds of bamboo and if one dies it doesn't ruin the whole effect."

The exotic look: orienpet lilies snared in the giant foliage of mayapple, banana, and tetrapanax, against a background of mixed bamboos.

Linda's special world is certainly not typical of the Pacific Northwest coast garden. It neither reflects nor draws upon the indigenous landscape for its inspiration. It reflects Linda's vision and taste, which, it is fair to say, are radical. It works so well because once you step past the bullfrog and through the gate, the world outside is entirely shut out. Wherever you stand, in whatever direction you look, all you see is Linda's handiwork—groves of bamboo, the "clash of the Titans," perimeter trees, bits of wall, the house itself. There are no views beyond, no neighbouring house or garden, no native forest, no sight of the sea. There are no "borrowed landscapes" to be incorporated. Linda's garden is an entirely enclosed, private space—an inspired space.

A preview of Linda's ideal future, arranged on her patio—a portable pot garden of drought-tolerant plants, such as cycads, agaves, cacti, and echeverias.

"WHEN YOU GARDEN, you're creating something that's visually interesting, in the way a painting might be. But that's a fixed point in time, like a picture in a gardening book. A garden has another dimension, and that's *time*. That's something I think about a lot—about how something's going to look over time. How it will change, and how I will change.

"Once in a while, I think, 'Wouldn't it be nice to just carry on here.' But, on the other hand, this place is really too big for me to take care of, because I do it all myself. David is really not a gardening kind of a guy. He's not a handy kind of a guy. I don't want him to come out with a chainsaw, like my father once did, and ask, 'Do you want any weeding done?'

"For the future, my ideal garden would have a large courtyard, with a lot of beautiful pots of all sizes, filled with the plants I love. And water, too. And that's it. No lawn, no beds, no borders. A garden that I could change and rearrange and, when I wanted, would let me just take off and not worry about it."

The Kennedys' enchanted house and garden, enveloped by forest and foliage.

TEN

The Gift to Be Free

Hydrangeas snuggle together. PHOTO DES KENNEDY

THE DAWNING OF THE MODERN Age of Aquarius inspired a wave of long-haired idealists to explore alternative lifestyles across the land. In the late 1960s and early 1970s, British Columbia's Gulf Islands were a popular magnet for back-to-the-landers, and Des and Sandy Kennedy were among them. Escaping demanding jobs in Vancouver, they used their savings to buy almost eleven acres on Denman Island, ten minutes by ferry to Vancouver Island, near Courtenay. While some of those pioneers eventually returned to the cities, jobs, and lives they'd fled, the Kennedys stayed on Denman.

Situated in a natural bowl and fenced against deer, their half-acre garden is a thing of mature beauty. The surrounding stone walls and paths, the fairy-tale, hand-hewn house and outbuildings, the trellises, fences, ponds, and patios are not only the fruits of more than forty years of their labour but are also made mostly from materials found either on site or elsewhere on the island. Their achievement is "an ecology of enchantment," which is also the title of Des's 1998 book. In late June, after a long, very cool spring, the Kennedys' garden was starting to warm up with birdsong, fragrance, and emerging blossom everywhere.

"Wild exuberance, I love that," says Sandy. "We like the plants to snuggle together—purposefully."

For Des and Sandy, gardening is a joint and shared obsession. Throughout

Back-to-the-landers Des and Sandy Kennedy, with their dog, Yuma. The cabin now serves as a writing studio. PHOTOS KENNEDY ARCHIVES

our garden tour and lunch, and always in two-part harmony, they told their story, and not for the first time. Des is a successful memoirist, satirist, novelist, garden writer, and speaker. Usually, it is his *pen* that has recorded the eventful progress of the garden—the frustrations and setbacks, the plagues and pests, and, most of all, the sheer pleasure of its history.

As Des remembers it, he and Sandy were immediately charmed when they saw the property for the first time in 1971. "The real estate agent started us off at the far end, with its beautiful, big, mature second-growth forest. We went down this amazing hillside, following a little creek. There were sword ferns in the undergrowth and conifers—big Doug firs and cedars—with skunk cabbages blooming in the creek. We walked back up—enchanted. This was just the most beautiful little place we'd ever seen. The creek splashing over mossy stones, birds everywhere. Goodness!

"The agent was very canny, because the last bit we saw was the area that's now at the entrance to the property, where the vegetable garden is. It had all been completely clear-cut. And the part in behind us, where our so-called arboretum is now, that was also hacked to bits, with all the trees felled and abandoned on the ground—an ugly, big tangle of slash and garbage. That was the top and perimeter. Down here it was all big alder trees, most at the end of their lives, and maybe five big western red cedars.

"So first we literally had to cut our way in from the road through piles of slash. We cleared the land as best we could with no heavy equipment. That meant hacking and burning and digging out stumps with axes and grub hoes. We must have burned out dozens and dozens of big stumps. But, we were young—twenty-six or twenty-seven."

Young, yes, and strong and determined. Nonetheless, Des and Sandy were literally babes in the woods when it came to sodbusting skills.

On Denman Island, a deer-proof fence is essential.

"Our vision was we would live here, grow our own food, and raise our own animals," says Des. "I would make a few bucks writing and life would be good, which turned out to be exactly what happened. But the first year was rough. In the spring, we built a little ten-by-eight-foot shack, long since gone, made pretty much by hand out of deadfall alder logs and such. It started with a plastic roof, then a shake roof. It was freezing cold—we might as well have been living outdoors, even though we had a woodstove. This was roughing it in the worst kind of way. We used to put bricks in the oven of the woodstove, heat them, put them in the bed, and jump in quickly because it was so bloody cold. But that gave us horrible chilblains. I'd had them as a kid in England, where we'd all put our feet right onto the coal-fire hearth. Sounds Dickensian, doesn't it?

"Then we started on a larger cabin nearby, thinking we would get into that for the first winter. We had very little money, but I remember that first dwelling cost us around a hundred and twenty dollars in cash. We moved in just before Christmas, and lived there for seven years, very happily." An early animal companion was their dog, Yuma. "Reputedly, he was part wolf," says Des. "He was the best defence we've ever had against deer and other marauders."

When you enter their property from Pickles Road, a gently winding drive takes you past that little cabin, which now serves as Des's writing studio. Vehicles are left up top and you meander down into the fenced garden and toward a lovely house of whimsical design, an artful arrangement of roofs and gables. Garden

Above: Walls, terraces, and pathways of sandstone slabs throughout the garden. "The Sisyphean folly of it!"

Below: Found art, sculpted by wind and wave.

beds surround the house. Outside the fence, a swath of lawn takes the eye up to further woodland and beyond. Within the garden, well-pruned shrubs and small trees, perennials, and grasses are massed in terraced beds, which undulate downward in waves of foliage and bloom. Walls and steps of local sandstone enclose the beds and provide year-round warmth to the garden.

"Rock has always been Des's passion," Sandy observes. "For years and years, we'd go along Pickles Road, following the road grader. As it unearthed rocks, we'd gather them up. Actually, Des was the primary hauler. I hate working with rocks—they're a very hard medium. But he loves it. We look at them now and say, 'How in the world did we move them all?'"

"By hand," Des replies. "From Pickles Road down here to this garden, only to push them back uphill to make the walls. We could have rolled them *down* into place. The Sisyphean folly of it!"

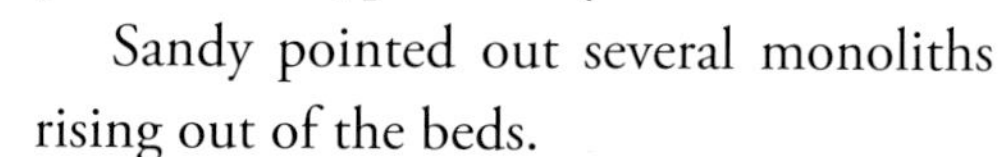

Sandy pointed out several monoliths rising out of the beds.

"Those are new rock structures, there. In the winter they just glisten over everything. Des calls these 'standing stones.' I think the rockwork gives this garden its island identity and some antiquity. In the winter, when they shine with moisture on the moss, it's pure magic!"

"We thought we were cursed with that hill when we first started gardening here,"

PHOTO DES KENNEDY

says Des. "But it's a wonderful thing to have for a whole bunch of reasons: it gives you those layers all up and down, and you can see the garden from so many different aspects. You're surrounded by your garden and also able to look up into it."

"Furthermore," adds Sandy, "looking *down* into a garden is thrilling. Look down now, right into those dogwood blossoms. They're much fuller and richer when you can see whole ribbons of them from this higher perspective. So what was once a wasted area, full of thistles and stumps, has turned into this beautiful, wondrous landscape."

The Kennedys' garden is designed for viewing, with chairs and benches placed carefully here and there to capture the eye and offer rest. Sandy calls them "stations of the cross" chairs.

"We sit somewhere different, depending on the time of year and the time of day. Wherever the current, most exciting spot is, we'll take a drink at the end of the day and sit and wonder at the beauty of the garden."

"And, if you'll pardon the expression, we are quite religious about taking Sundays off, because generally we work six days a week. So we've created pleasant nooks for reading and relaxing," Des explains. "I'm frequently amazed to go into other gardens and find one hard little bench. It's an amazing oversight. The Chinese are so wise in insisting that garden design includes multiple stops to pause, enjoy, sit, meditate."

In the early 1970s, when the Kennedys began taming their new wilderness, garden walls, beds, and plants—the very concept of ornamental gardening—were far off the "to-do" list. Survival was uppermost in their minds; immediate

Looking down into the dogwood blossoms (*Cornus kousa chinensis*). PHOTO DES KENNEDY

self-sufficiency, their credo. First, they concentrated on creating a vegetable garden, an orchard, chicken runs, and a goat shed. Beautification was limited, as Des describes in his 2010 memoir, *The Way of a Gardener*, to a "scattering of daffodils, planted before we even had a proper roof over our heads."[1]

THOUGH THEY BOTH came from gardening families, neither Des nor Sandy was familiar with the coastal BC landscape or its exuberant growing potential. Des was born in a working-class neighbourhood of Liverpool and emigrated with his family in the mid-1950s.

"My dad gardened professionally in England. When we moved to Toronto, the first thing he did was tear out everything on our little city lot. The whole front garden became ornamentals, while the back was turned into vegetables and fruits—not a square inch of anything else. We were a family with four boys, and what we wanted was a lawn with room to throw a ball, but no space whatsoever was kept for that! And I paid *no* attention to my dad's gardening. My mum kept an eye on it and processed the food—the classic story: he grew it, she cooked it.

"I can't believe how hard they worked. He was a technician on the Toronto subway system. He worked the night shift, came home and immediately went off to a local greenhouse-cum-nursery for another four hours or so. Then home to tend his own gardens, sleep a few hours, and back to the TTC—day after day after day, the same routine. He was a little Irishman, barely over five feet tall, full of vigour and a grouch. So the last thing we wanted was to have anything to do with him—the gardener, or his garden. Now, I regret that.

Des and Sandy Kennedy.

"Then I went off to the monastic seminary when I was sixteen. There was little gardening involved at all. When I left at the age of twenty-three and came to Vancouver, I didn't garden there either. Not until I met Sandy in the late 1960s. We loved camping together—camping was what inspired the decision to move to the country. We married in 1970, bought this property in '71, and we moved here full-time in '72."

"My gardening backstory is quite different," says Sandy. "I grew up on a farm near Edmonton. My father was Ukrainian, my mother English. My early and definitive memory is of all our Ukrainian neighbours gathering to do what amounted to communal gardening. They'd travel by horse and cart, and arrive at our farm with their whisky bottles, their fiddles, and their accordions. They grew and picked things such as cabbage, onions, potatoes, and beets to store over the winter. As young kids, we'd all be there around the huge vegetable garden. There would be dancing and singing and eating. In the garden, there were weeds all over the place, but we would manage to grow huge amounts of everything in that wonderful prairie soil. I grew up eating food grown where I lived. I just took it for granted.

"When I went away to Dalhousie University, I saw the other kinds of gardens people made, and smaller farms, too. Then I came to UBC for graduate work, moved into social work, and met Des. I was a natural candidate for the back-to-the-land movement, which for us, as Des said, grew out of the pleasure we shared while camping in nature. We both had promising careers and were doing really innovative stuff in our field—films, travelling around and doing various kinds of artistic projects, and winning awards. When we left our jobs, people were horrified. They'd ask, 'Why are you giving all that up to move to a remote island?' Because it was true, Denman was very remote. But even then we had come to the important realization that we wanted to tread gently upon the Earth. We were seeking a life where we could grow our own food, and live in and with nature."

Was their back-to-the-land resolve ever shaken? Tested, yes, they say. The solution? "We'd take a day off and go into town, maybe once every couple of months. We'd get a motel room, bring in fast food, and watch junk TV. Somehow that resolved the temporary frustration. Otherwise, we were really fired up with what we were building. For me, the work was part of my heritage, from my hardy Ukrainian pioneering stock," says Sandy.

"A great sense of freedom settled over us when we moved to Denman," says Des. "After a day's work here, we'd sit around a campfire with friends, drink homemade wine, smoke dope, and plan the next day's work. Other than the building stuff, at which we were all complete neophytes, it was stress-free. All my life to that point had been under stressful, demanding, guilt-inducing circumstances. This new freedom carried me a long, long way. There was also a really wonderful young community here—a community of wandering PHDs and various characters pursuing the alternative lifestyle. Some drifted away; others stayed, including us."

Political engagement came with their growing commitment to the island lifestyle. As Des and Sandy witnessed first the indiscriminate logging of parts of Denman Island, then logging threats to old-growth forests on Vancouver Island, they joined the organized protests. Coincidentally, their political involvement went hand in hand with garden building.

Sandy says, "I owe a debt of gratitude to friends who, every year, would send us a gardens-beautiful calendar from Britain. I'd look at the pictures and think, 'Goodness, if we could create even a tinge of that beauty here, it would be wonderful.' Never at that point did I dream that we would have anything like those English gardens. But the images certainly stayed with me. I remember how the garden started: we'd finished building the house and we took off for Europe for a year, and then shortly after we returned, we starting putting in little beds."

Des agrees. "Yes, that trip to Europe was pivotal. We'd literally just cobbled this house together by hook and by crook, and we had a little tiny space out front for a garden, but nothing of real interest was growing there.

"During our trip, we visited many of the great estate gardens in England—the National Trust gardens and others. That's when we began to understand what it was to have a really beautiful created surrounding—like the calendar pictures Sandy mentioned. Somehow that series of events made us realize that we shouldn't just sit in the woods. We were going to create a garden. The vegetable gardening and orchard had been happening for almost ten years and continued. But the inspiration to make a beautiful, expansive garden started then.

"Camping on Corfu, we became aware that the whole mountainside was terraced. We would walk those stony paths every day. We got home and confronted this impossible space. This hill had been logged and only a few spindly alder trees were left, with blackberries and brambles filling in with a vengeance. We'd made a couple of efforts at planting—a shrub here and there, a tamarisk tree because we'd fallen in love with one we saw up the Island Highway. But the terraces on Corfu were the *aha!* moment. We started gathering stones and trucked in—we counted—between seventy and eighty loads of rock. We built the walls first and started in on the beds. And, yes, as Sandy said, that was right around the time of the Strathcona Provincial

Blowsy climbing roses 'Albertine' and 'Madame Grégoire Staechelin'.

Park blockade in 1988. It was one of those times of manic, frenzied energy, politically and horticulturally. We'd be away at the blockade, then return and work on building this hill garden."

By this time, though Des had started earning some money through freelance magazine writing, the garden was kept on a low, low budget.

"A lot was grown from seed or from cuttings, stuff people gave us, a lot of native plants, a lot of reduced-for-quick-sale items at the nurseries, or salvaged from dumpsters. It's astonishing—if you went to a nursery now to try and duplicate this, you'd lay out a whole pile of money. I won't say it cost us nothing, but next to nothing. The hardscape and stones were local and free; all the wood structures were split from red cedar logs found in the forest. Initially, the plants were simple, showy, hardy performers—foxgloves, hollyhocks, and a lot of semi-weeds such as daisies—nothing sophisticated."

Rosa 'Kiftsgate'.
PHOTO
DES KENNEDY

Sandy remembers one major purchase. "Some plants we wanted right from the beginning. The roses, for instance, were our first big buy. We chose old roses, fifty or sixty of them at two bucks apiece."

Other guiding principles were pragmatic. "We encouraged a lot of native plants, which, along with the stone and cedar, knit the garden into its forest setting. That's also why we left all the big cedar stumps. So many people bulldoze them out. I've seen concrete 'cedar' stumps in Vancouver, for heaven's sake. Also, water-wise gardening was a part of the equation right from the beginning. At first, unknowingly, we put in plants that were real water-gobblers and found that in the heat of the summer, we had to water them literally every day. Another first principle was to create a wildlife-friendly garden, to attract the butterflies and birds and so forth. And fragrance, fragrance, fragrance. What we would do is buy one plant—a honeysuckle, for example—and then layer

it to get ten honeysuckles. That's how a lot of plants multiplied around here."

Thus, the charming cottage garden described in Des's early books, such as *Crazy About Gardening* (1994) and *An Ecology of Enchantment* (1998), grew to become a gently sculpted garden, shaped and clipped into complementary patterns and waves of colour.

Sandy continues, "Each of these sculpted shrubs initially began as a tiny thing that's now grown into its own. The evolution of this garden is written in patience—the patience to know that these little evergreen things could eventually become the green architecture. Having read countless English gardening books, we knew that the blowsiness of the flowering plants would have to be balanced and grounded."

Top: Yellow is welcomed in the Kennedys' garden.

Opposite: After forty years of building their garden, Des and Sandy appreciate plants that look after themselves. Top to bottom: *Hydrangea petiolaris*, the very fragrant cottage pink (*Dianthus plumarius*), *Thalictrum aquilegifolium*.

"But we also had to unlearn some of the stuff we read," Des adds. "For instance, denouncing the colour yellow in the garden, as one so-called expert advised. We came to realize that this is not really an English climate, even though we can grow a lot of the same things. The quality of light here is very different, so the delicate pastels don't work for us, at least not for long in the July sun. But who can resist this combination of *Lysimachia punctata*, with Jerusalem sage and spiderwort?

"But overall, we structured this garden to mirror what makes up the forest: establishing a canopy with a lot of shrubs underneath, and many different plants below, like the layers of the forest. The garden flows with the land and I think that distinguishes it from gardens built on a level surface. As we age, we're moving more and more toward structural plants and grasses and away from maintaining such a wide variety of growth. We're gradually eliminating the things that take a lot of work, such as the big herbaceous stuff."

Sandy picks up on the topic of aging. "We talk about it all the time! That's why we built the new sunroom and created a level entry. We want to live here as long as possible, and preferably die here. My fantasy is that I'll lie in my little bed in the sunroom; the roses will take over, and the garden will be bursting with serendipitous growth and be absolutely stunning. My rational wish is that we can just let it do what it will do, and continue to live in its beauty."

"Yes indeed," agrees Des. "Then I like to imagine this all going back to forest again. It wouldn't take long; just turn your back. We've been here forty years. We came as kids and built everything you see out of a piece of raw land. That doubles and triples the significance of this place for us. All our blood and sweat and toil poured into it, which makes it very difficult to consider its future, or its end, or its transformation. We talk about passing it on to a conservancy. But on the other hand, wouldn't it be great if another young couple had the chance to do here what we did?"

"That would be a real gift to leave," says Sandy.

Glen Patterson's extraordinary garden viewed from inside his third-floor apartment.

ELEVEN

The Man Who Loves Conifers

IN VANCOUVER'S WEST END, WALK down Jervis Street toward Coal Harbour, and as you pass Pender Street, look up. You'll see the tops of twenty-foot pines and maples growing in Glen Patterson's third-floor roof garden. It's a wonder of engineering and horticultural imagination. There's nothing like it anywhere else in the city.

The first glimpse from the street provokes curiosity. The first visit provokes amazement. For this is not the usual rooftop or balcony garden—a collection of tubs, pots, window boxes, containers of wood, clay, or plastic. This is a two-thousand-square-foot rock garden, exquisitely laid out in the Japanese style, with rock ranging from pebbles to boulders the size of an industrial fridge, pathways and walls: a landscape that's home to a collector's array of precisely arranged plants. Hundreds of plants. To complete its perfection, there's a flowing stream with pools up to three feet deep, where large gold and silver koi circle lazily in the dappled shade of overhanging conifers and maples. It just happens to be thirty feet above ground, and it is entered from Glen's apartment through glass doors.

Many passionate gardeners, contemplating the relentless advance of old age and decrepitude, accept with sad resignation that, one day, they will be forced to move to smaller, more manageable quarters and leave it all behind. Not Glen Patterson. One day in 1997, as a widower in his late seventies, he surveyed his one-acre garden in West Vancouver. He saw all he had accomplished: a garden famous for its collection of rare plants; the Japanese-style framework of pines and maples; the cascading pools, rock gardens, and pathways. It was, he reflected, the culmination of a lifetime of gardening and he'd be damned if he'd leave it behind. He would take it with him, albeit on a smaller scale. And he had the means to do it—the rewards of a life of determination, hard work, and great success in the British Columbia forest industry. He also had the motivation of a lifelong gardener.

"My earliest memories as a little boy in Calgary are of going over to my grandmother's place and helping her thin carrots and leeks. This would be in the mid-1920s. I remember she had a deep, cool cellar where she stored all the root vegetables and preserved fruit for the winter. I'd climb down the ladder with her. I remember she knew how to keep carrots in sand so they wouldn't sprout. And she kept eggs in water glass. Awful stuff—but the eggs didn't go bad."

Glen took a commerce degree before the war, then joined the Royal Canadian Air Force and trained as a pilot. In 1945, after victory in Europe and demobilization, he moved to Vancouver, where his childhood sweetheart, Isobel, joined him, and they soon married. But there were no jobs. So Glen considered the career prospects in BC and astutely decided that forestry offered the best future and that the best way to ensure he had a piece of it would be to take a second degree, in forestry.

"While I was a student, Isobel and I couldn't afford our own place. We lived for two years in a boarding house. Just one room. Shared bathroom. And even with two degrees, I couldn't get any work, not even labouring work. The Depression mentality hung on. However, one of my professors was conducting a survey of forests at the northern end of Vancouver Island and could take a couple of summer students. 'You come,' he said to me. 'But what about my wife? I can't think of leaving her.' Well, it turned out they needed a temporary cook at the camp up there, so Isobel got that job and off we went."

This was Woss Camp, run by the forestry giant Canadian Forest Products Ltd. (now Canfor). After the survey was completed, the company needed a timekeeper and wanted Isobel to stay on.

"Of course they had to take me too. They gave us a little house and we decided we'd like to start a garden. But there was no soil. All rock and gravel.

So every day when I was off timber cruising or whatever, I'd carry out a couple of gunnysacks of soil—wet, sour, swamp soil. I was strong in those days. And we spread that over the gravel and in a few weeks had enough to start a lawn. Then we wanted flowers. So I dug out rocks, hauled in more soil, and made a border around the lawn. Now, Isobel loved dahlias. The bigger, the better. Twelve, thirteen inches across. All colours. Then I made window boxes and filled them with big colourful begonias we bought on trips to Vancouver. What a show! And we painted the house. The union didn't like it—us fixing up the company house, growing a garden. They feared the company would make everyone do it!

"Then Canfor wanted me to study and plan the long-term harvesting of timber in the Nimpkish Valley. Sustained yield was the buzzword, a brand-new idea in those days. I was the first professional forester hired. I loved that work. It got me out into nature and I learned an awful lot about the trees, especially conifers, and their requirements."

Next, the company offered him a management position in Vancouver.

"We leapt at the idea. We'd saved up some money in the nine years at Woss Camp and bought city property on a hill, with great views of the ocean and the mountains. We had three children by then. And of course we couldn't wait to have a garden."

More dahlias?

"No. No more dahlias. Roses. We joined the Rose Society. We were simply over the moon about roses. We competed in the shows. We brought in the latest, the best, prizewinning roses from England. We pored over catalogues and brought in the best from the States. We had a wonderful garden, the talk of the town. Even today I occasionally take my grandchildren to see it."

In 1956, Glen, then thirty-five, was offered a senior position, based in Grande Prairie, Alberta. He would be in charge of company operations and mills over a large territory. The country around was farmland, with deep clay. In summer there was plenty of sun and eighteen hours of daylight.

"We made a new garden up there. Nobody else bothered. They'd plant out a few petunias or geraniums in summer. That was all. We concentrated on alpines—that was the start of a great interest of mine, which I've built on ever since. At that latitude, the climate was like being five thousand feet high further south, like Banff and Lake Louise, which were in my backyard when I was a child. There were no rocks in the area, but I collected them where I could and sent away for plants or picked them up at nurseries wherever we could find them. And I learned a lot about the special conditions alpine plants need."

IN THE 1960S, under Glen's leadership, Canfor's fortunes in the north much improved and he was appointed vice-president of northern operations, with an office in the Vancouver headquarters. For Isobel, it was paradise regained. They found an old house in Southlands, near the Fraser River. A stream ran through the property, its steep banks forested with old-growth Douglas firs. There was a dogwood in front of the house.

"The biggest I've ever seen. It bloomed its heart out every year." And what then, roses? "No roses, no dahlias. We became crazy for rhododendrons. We joined the Rhododendron Society.

"Then came the great tragedy of my whole life. My dear wife, Isobel. She died. Breast cancer. Even now, after some forty years, it brings a lump in my throat to talk about it. I still think of her every day.

"It had such an impact on me, I just couldn't stay there. So I bought a place in West Vancouver. This was an acre lot with lawns at every level and beds that had to be weeded all the time. The people before me had a full-time gardener. And I realized that I could manage without one if the garden could be simplified. So I went to the Department of Botany at UBC and I said, 'I'm getting older, I want to have a garden that's beautiful but without all this work and a place that would be friendly and welcoming. What do I do?' 'Well,' they said, 'go Asian.'

"I'd been to Japan and I knew what they meant. I was captivated, *captivated*, by the beauty of Japanese styling. Those Kyoto temple gardens. I still dream about them, they're so enchanting. They're easy-care and they have meaning. A lawn over there would be an obscenity."

At this time, Glen briefly resumed life as a student and, in California, took a course in landscape design, based on the principles of Owen Dell, particularly the concept of *sustainability*. As Dell wrote, "Think about the things you'd rather not have to do in your garden and consider whether there may be a way

Glen's passion for alpine plants, conifers, and the Japanese style are brought together in his garden.

to eliminate them . . . For some it's weeding, for others it might be shearing the hedges or mowing the lawn, but in all cases it's some part of the gardening experience that is tedious, disheartening and minimally rewarding."[1]

For Glen, the course was life-changing.

"Well, the lawns had to come out. Even a small lawn. Every week it's got to be cut. It's all work, work, work, work. And for what purpose? If your kids need grass to play on, send them to the park, I say. That's what they're for. All that grass was added to the compost heap. Then you have plants like roses. They have to be watered and pruned and fertilized constantly and sprayed for pests and diseases. After that course, I took all the roses and threw them in the compost. I threw them all out and along with them, all that constant work."

THE ROOFTOP GARDEN above Jervis Street is an alpine garden, the fulfillment of Glen's passion for conifers and alpine plants. That day in 1997 when he decided to move and take his garden with him, appreciating the realities of living alone into his eighties and beyond, he knew he had to find a home on one level, with easy access to buses and taxis, restaurants, and a hospital.

The happy rocks.

He had to live in the city. An apartment would suit him, but what about his garden? He learned of plans for a waterfront condo development that included a high-rise block with a two-storey, flat-roofed townhouse attached on the east side. Glen grasped the possibility of using its roof as a garden, which could be stepped into from a third-floor apartment. He met the architect and won him over.

There followed two years of planning and consultation with engineers and the project manager, and arm-twisting and negotiation with city hall, eventually resulting in approval to reinforce the townhouse roof with steel beams sufficient to bear 275 tons, roughly the equivalent of 185 small cars. For waterproofing and drainage, a multi-layer sandwich was laid down, with ten sheets of rubber interspersed with filtering and insulation materials. Glen now had a two-thousand-square-foot canvas on which to paint his garden. He mixed his pigments on principles inspired by Asian tradition.

"For me, there are five important things the garden needs. First, every garden must have *water*. It's a part of gardening that's a *must*. The calmness of it. If you sit quietly there, the birds will come in and preen their feathers and drink from the pool. Then you must have *space*. Open enough so the spirits can live. Most gardeners jam all the plants together and let them grow, and next thing you know it's a jungle.

"You need good *rocks* and the rocks have to be placed beautifully. I've got a gardener, Jim Nakano, who trained in Japan in the Zen tradition. In their belief, rocks have a spirit and—I know it sounds crazy—but they have to be happy. You don't just tumble rocks together. You fit them. You have to find the right rocks and move them, separate them, lean them, step back, and when it looks right, then you put the plants in. The rocks come first.

"I learned that lesson some years ago. In West Vancouver, I had all these beautiful hostas, different kinds, and I said to Jim, 'I want to put them in this area here. They'll make a lovely display, all different shades of leaf colour.' So I left him to it and came back half an hour later. There wasn't a single plant in place! He was setting rocks in there, moving them around, trying this and that, and once he was satisfied, he put the plants in, carefully selecting the right place

Carnivorous pitcher plants (*Sarracenia species*).

High-rise towers form an imposing backdrop to the garden.

for each one. What a knockout it was! And I suddenly realized I couldn't have done that, but the way he did it couldn't be better. He's been an inspiration for me.

"Then of course you have to have *plants*. And they have to be plants that fit with the rocks and the water and of course the space. That is so important. The foreground balanced with the distance. You can make a small garden look vast simply by the placement of plants with different shapes and sizes and colours.

"And on top of all that you must have *pathways* that go around and through the garden. The layout of the pathways must be designed to give you anticipation, excitement, mystery, like animal pathways in nature. You create surprises. You walk so far and the pathway stops, or suddenly a whole new view opens up, like a borrowed landscape from the scenery beyond the garden."

Rock defines all the dimensions of Glen's garden: the contours, the heights, and the depths. It forms the framework in walls, steps, and pathways, in pools with three small waterfalls, and in carefully sited boulders—all planned and placed to give the space a natural look.

Water cascading over artificial rock screened by *Rhododendron quinquefolium* and an azalea in bloom.

"Actually, this is artificial rock. I wanted to have the same kind of rock I had in West Vancouver. It was so beautiful. But how could I get it up here? It was too heavy. Impossible. Then I noticed the Vancouver Aquarium had beautiful sculpted artificial rock. You couldn't tell the difference. That eventually led me to a fellow called Paul who did this sort of thing, and I liked his work and hired him. For this project, he took on two young graduates from the Emily Carr art school. These people made frames with rebar and wire mesh. They bent it and shaped it. Then there was a truck down below and a special mix of concrete, pumped up through a six-inch pipe. Paul held the pipe and spread the mix over the mesh, about an inch thick, with the artists moulding and shaping as they went along. I was there giving a little advice—'The steps here could be

This hundred-and-twenty-year-old maple was dug up and hoisted to the rooftop and, amazingly, survived the ordeal.

a little wider, how about a little crevice here, a crack there to put some soil in and get rid of that artificial look.' Then when it was all done, he came in two or three times and spray-painted it to make it look like rock. Now, some years later, there's moss and lichen growing on it. It's naturalized. You can't tell the difference. You know, I think people who want rock in their gardens might do that, instead of going out into the woods and trying to wrestle big blocks of granite home in the back of a pickup.

"Oh, look, there's a robin having a bath. And over there, another one. That's its mate. They're here all the time. It will come right up to me. And its song is absolutely thrilling. We have flocks of finches here at certain times of year. It's like an oasis, isn't it, a natural space in the middle of this urban setting."

TWO YEARS BEFORE the move from West Vancouver to the rooftop, Glen consulted soil experts and began to experiment with different mixes to determine the optimum medium. It should weigh as little as possible and provide good drainage while retaining moisture. It should be rich in humus. He chose a mix of black pumice, graded sand, and coconut fibre. At the same time, he

The black pine. Boxwood in the foreground, "pruned properly."

and his gardener, Jim Nakano, began to select and prepare the plants that would be moved to the new site, especially the most precious and risky transplants: the favourite trees—pines, maples, rarities all. A maple (*Acer palmatum dissectum atropurpureum*), which Glen reckoned to be a hundred and twenty years old, presented a particularly risky challenge.

"It weighed about three thousand pounds when it was moved here. The architect said we couldn't have anything more than a three-foot-diameter hole, so two years before it was moved, Jim cut the fifteen-foot spreading roots down to a diameter of just three feet and then dug a trench all round which he filled with sawdust and bark mulch. Then I had to keep it well watered for two years so it grew all these fine new root hairs. Finally it was lifted out of the ground with a clamshell sort of device, loaded onto a truck, and then hoisted by crane to the rooftop. Amazingly, it survived and just look at it now."

Thirty-three tons of the special soil mixture were mixed and spread across the rocky landscape. Sixteen and a half tons of water filled the pools. The selected trees and shrubs, including the maple, were moved overnight on three flatbed trucks. At dawn the following day, installation began. That happened at the end of the second millennium. Now, twelve years into the third, Glen shows visitors around with a great deal of entirely justifiable pride.

"This is a sustainable garden. Sustainability to me means that once you've achieved your artistic concept, you keep it that way without aggressive cost and work. There's no lawn to cut or hedges to trim. There are no raccoons or deer or even slugs. Watering is automatic. I don't use any fertilizer. All that does is create excessive soft growth which has to be cut back. I don't spray chemicals. The only thing that has to be done is keep the trees pruned and once a year, we do a thorough weeding."

The centrepiece of Glen's garden is a black pine, *Pinus thunbergii*, nearly fifteen feet high.

The blue Japanese pine, *Pinus parviflorus.*

"I've had it for over thirty years, all along pruned in the Japanese style. Once a year Jim climbs up to give it a trim and keep it looking that way. This basic structure and style have been carried on in other trees here. Such as over there. Can you think of anything more ugly than the hedge the English use everywhere—boxwood, all geometric, rectangular, totally boring. Now there's a boxwood pruned properly. Isn't it a beauty? It's got a nice stem and you can see through it. An Englishman would die if he saw that, because it's not a box at all!"

We noted that Glen uses "English" as a term of general disparagement for a garden style that includes lawns, clipped hedges, bedding plants, and herbaceous borders—anything that in his view imposes on nature rather than working with it.

"Here's the blue Japanese pine, *Pinus parviflorus*. Pruned this way, you can see the bones and the bluish foliage, but look, here's one branch that's left long and stretches over the pool at least twelve feet. That's to keep the herons out. It looks perfectly natural and I don't need to stretch wires over the water, which is so unattractive.

Above left: The bustling Vancouver harbour.

Above right: *Acer palmatum* 'Koto No Ito'.

"And of course in this location, where the trees are necessarily shallow-rooted and the root ball has been restricted, the wind has to blow easily through. They scarcely move in a strong wind. If this was just a jungle of untamed foliage, the whole thing would be too top-heavy and could blow off the roof in the first big storm. And the light can get through into my windows and in all seasons I can sit in my living room there and see through the garden to all the variations in colour and weather, to the mountains and all the harbour activity, the cruise ships, and the tugs plying back and forth."

Glen delights in his garden, and his enthusiasm is infectious.

"Now here's one of the most beautiful Japanese maples there is. You know what I love about the Japanese? They don't name a thing after places or people; they name it after what it looks like. They call this one 'Koto No Ito,' which means 'old harp with fine strings.' Isn't that apt? Isn't that lovely? Look how feathery it is."

He continued the tour against a tuneful background of birdsong and tinkling water, a peaceful scene occasionally interrupted by the roar of a float plane taking off like an angry hornet, an aggravation reminding us that we were in the heart of the city. He called our attention to his collection of alpine plants, scores of them, and the events in his life that encouraged this passion.

"My eldest son, Dennis, graduated in law and moved to the Arctic. Eventually he became premier of the Northwest Territories. Now he's the senator for Nunavut. He married an Inuk woman and his family grew up there. I would visit often and saw all these wonderful plants. You've never seen anything like it. Take *Rhododendron lapponicum*, for example, the Lapland rosebay. You'd see great drifts of it, blooming just as soon as the sun had

melted the snow and thawed just the top two inches of permafrost. That's all it needed. Only three inches high. And fragrant, which is rare among rhododendrons. I just *had* to have that in my West Vancouver garden. I had good soil. It would be happy there. So I asked one of my grandsons to dig some up and bring them to me. Chose a good spot. Planted it. Kept it moist. No good. It died. Where did I go wrong? Ah! The soil. It needs its native soil, minerals and all that. So next time I said to my grandson, 'Bring me a bag of soil with the plant.' Same thing. It died. So what now? Companion plants. That's what it needs. So I said, 'Bring me anything growing nearby, grasses, whatever.' Same thing. No luck. Nobody has ever been able to grow that little purple rhododendron in the garden. Those Arctic plants are exactly tuned to their harsh environment, hugging the ground, which is a degree or two warmer than the air in the growing season. They don't want to be anywhere else. They don't want an easy life.

Alpine treasures tucked into holes and crevices bored into soft tufa rock. This collection sits on the floor of the roof garden, but no container can be seen. One of Glen's innovations is wrapping a bed of tufa and soil in landscape cloth, its edges cleverly concealed by plants, rocks, and gravel.

Glen feeding his pets.

"It's a great challenge to grow alpines here. The conditions in Vancouver are so different from the Arctic or six thousand feet up Mount Baker, say. I found one of the best ways to meet the challenge is to use tufa rock. It's volcanic, very light and soft, drains well but holds moisture. So you can easily make a hole, put a little plant in. The roots find their way into the pores of the rock. They're totally happy. Right plant in the right place. That's a principle every gardener should observe. I find even miniature conifers do well in tufa.

"I have a great affection for conifers. There are so many varieties and shapes and sizes, and in the wintertime they're still beautiful with their foliage. There's a mix of dwarf conifers here. This little spruce I've had for half a century. It's *Picea glauca* 'Laurin'. It grows a quarter of an inch a year. It's only grown about a foot in the fifty years I've had it."

It was time to feed the koi their daily ration of pellets.

"These are my pets, you know. Aren't they pretty? I like the yellow ones best. Here's what I do to get their attention." Glen stirs the water with his cane. "Then they know it's feeding time. Those big ones there, I've had for twenty-five years or more. They'll eat right out of my hand. Look at them. Gobble, gobble. The little ones don't get a look-in.

"There you see lichen and moss growing naturally on this artificial rock, just as you'd find in nature. Here's another plant I want to show you: one of my favourites, *Rhododendron quinquefolium*, the five-leaf azalea from Japan. Ten years ago, Japanese Crown Prince Naruhito and his wife made *Rhododendron quinquefolium* the symbol of their newborn child, Princess Aiko. The whiteness of the flowers represented the pure heart of the infant princess. This is a very old one I got from a gardening friend who had a nursery up the Fraser Valley. I heard he was dying and visited him in his last days. He struggled around his garden with me and I saw a five-leaf azalea not properly planted and looking pretty sad, so I asked, 'What are you going to do with that?' and he said, 'Oh, I was going to sell it. You want it?' So he gave it to me."

Glen speaks of all of his plants as old friends. Many have a story attached.

"One of my favourite sites on Earth in the wild is up in the White Mountains in California, and there you have the bristlecone pine. It's amazing. Nothing else will grow there, at about twelve thousand feet. They're the oldest living thing on the planet. They found one that's fifty-five hundred years old. They're all gnarly and twisted and much of the bark is stripped, but they're alive! A friend took me up there to see them and I was just thrilled, so I went looking for a place to buy one and found a little nursery way up in the hills that specialized in native plants. She said, 'Oh, I'm not selling them now. I keep them until they're in gallon-sized pots.' I said, 'I'll pay you the one-gallon size,' and she sold me six. And here's one of them, *Pinus longaeva*.

"Now this one, you'll never see it in other gardens. Aesthetically, I think it is the best native conifer. It's a hemlock! A clone called 'Elizabeth'. It only grows at five thousand feet and higher along the coast of BC, lower down in the interior. I could have a garden just of conifers! I couldn't live without them. Look there, see that silvery blue against the tufa rock? I could go on and on about conifers, but I think you've heard enough."

Top: *Pinus longaeva*, the long-lived bristlecone pine.

Above: *Tsuga mertensiana* 'Elizabeth'. PHOTO GLEN PATTERSON

WE HAD BEEN treated to a retrospective of eighty years of Glen Patterson's gardening life—from helping his grandmother thin carrots to a sophisticated realization of the principles of the sustainable Asian garden, three floors above street level, so perfectly situated it might have dropped from heaven.

As we said goodbye, he handed over his camera and asked us to take his picture. He would be pasting this into a card and emailing it to all his family, inviting children, grandchildren, and great-grandchildren to join him in the garden to celebrate his ninetieth birthday, three months away. He looked well pleased.

Before that date, a trip east is booked, to attend an international rock garden convention and to photograph the alpine flora in the hills of New England. Glen will also, once again, cross the Arctic Circle to see the plants he loves, glowing brightly among the rocks and the lichen of the tundra in northern Scandinavia.

Ever the forward planner, he leaves little to chance. "This is my palliative care unit. I shall die here. It's all on one level. Even in a wheelchair I can be moved out into the garden, and I have an extra bedroom reserved for a full-time live-in nurse."

Beyond that, he has secured the garden's future. The owner of the town-house below, a man of considerable means, is a big admirer of Glen's rooftop creation and has bought the right of first refusal, following Glen's death, to purchase the apartment and the garden too. He wants to keep it just as it is, thus ensuring that, at least for the garden, there will be life after Glen's death.

Endnotes

OPENING QUOTATION

[1] Alexander Pope, *Epistles to Several Persons: Epistle IV To Richard Boyle, Earl of Burlington* (1731).

TWO: WINDCLIFF

[1] J.C. Raulston was an American plant collector and horticulturalist who, in Raleigh, North Carolina, founded the ten-acre botanical garden now named in his memory, the JC Raulston Arboretum. In 2009, reviewing Bobby Ward's biography of Dr. Raulston (*Chlorophyll in His Veins*), Dan Hinkley wrote, "Still to this day, after so many years, hardly a day passes without being reminded of J.C. There will be a plant encountered in the garden that he gave me, or mention of a book or film or something in the kitchen that brings him back briefly, fondly remembered."

[2] Shortly after our conversation, Heronswood was bought at auction by the Port Gamble S'Klallam Tribe, on whose ancestral land the property stands. According to Mother Nature Network, Dan Hinkley said "I couldn't be happier that the garden is back in the hands of people in the area who know the Pacific Northwest." Their goal, as described by the tribe's economic development coordinator, is "to improve and preserve the garden and to add native art and imagery to convey the history, and culture of the tribe."

[3] See www.flickr.com/photos/angusf/sets/656542.

SEVEN: A GARDEN IS A POEM

[1] Patrick Lane, *There is a Season: A Memoir* (Toronto: McClelland & Stewart, 2004), 202–203.

[2] Lorna Crozier, in *The Blue Hour of the Day: Selected Poems* (Toronto: McClelland & Stewart, 2007), 18; originally published in *The Garden Going On Without Us* (Toronto: McClelland & Stewart, 1985).

[3] Ibid., p. 26.

[4] Patrick Lane, *There is a Season*, 202.

EIGHT: STILL DREAMING OF PARADISE

[1] George Little and David Lewis, *A Garden Gallery* (Portland, OR: Timber Press, 2005), 18.

TEN: THE GIFT TO BE FREE

[1] Des Kennedy, *The Way of a Gardener: A Life's Journey* (Vancouver, BC: Greystone Books, 2010), 148.

ELEVEN: THE MAN WHO LOVES CONIFERS

[1] Owen Dell, *Pacific Horticulture*, Winter 1998.

Meconopsis 'Mrs Jebb' in authors' garden.

Plant Index

Acknowledgments

GARDENERS ARE THE FIRST TO extol the generosity of other gardeners, and this book owes everything to the generosity of those whose words we gathered as we toured their gardens, and whose hospitality we enjoyed on repeated visits. We were the grateful recipients of their many kindnesses. Not least, we thank them for their trust—there was nary a guarded trade secret among them.

Additionally, we are especially grateful to Beverley Merryfield, who encouraged and supported this project from the start and who also agreed to be interviewed, as did David Tarrant.

Others assisted us with introductions, photographs, and ideas. Our thanks to Erwin Diener, Judi Dyelle, Alex Fischer, Verity Goodier, Laurie Rolland, Angelina Seah, and Daniel Terry. David Goatley gave us his kind permission to reproduce his portrait of Robert Bateman.

Our travels took us away from home, garden, and our now dearly departed dog, Carlo. During those absences, he was cared for and consoled by kind friends Joan O'Brien, Jennifer Ingram, Shirley Anderson, and Nancy Webber.

Finally, we thank Ruth Linka, Emily Shorthouse, Pete Kohut, and Cailey Cavallin of TouchWood Editions, and our kind and fiercely competent editor, Marlyn Horsdal.

Carlo.